Martial Arts
Madness

Martial Arts
Madness
Light and Dark in the Esoteric Martial Arts

Glenn J. Morris

Frog, Ltd.
Berkeley, California

Published by Frog, Ltd.

Frog, Ltd. books are distributed by
North Atlantic Books
P.O. Box 12327
Berkeley, California 94712

Cover design by Paula Morrison
Book design by Catherine Campaigne

Printed in the United States of America

Library of Congress Cataloging-in-Publication Data

Morris, Glenn, 1944–
    Martial arts madness : a user's guide to the esoteric martial arts / Glenn Morris.
        p.   cm.
    Includes bibliographical references and index.
    ISBN 1-883319-77-3 (alk. paper)
    1. Martial arts—Psychological aspects.   I. Title.
GV1102.7.p75M87   1999
796.8'01'9—dc21   98-36693
                                                                        CIP

1   2   3   4   5   6   7   8   9   /   02   01   00   99   98

Contents

Foreword

In the spring of 1995 a student of mine, Wayne Oliver, asked if I was interested in meeting an "enlightened master of ninpo, the very person who could teach you the esoteric side of the martial arts." I had been an active martial artist for twenty-six years and had never met a single Master who could honestly teach anything to anyone about the spiritual/esoteric side of anything, much less the martial arts. I had been a police officer for eighteen years and had spent ten of those investigating "occult crimes," debunking spiritualists such as palm readers and crystal-ball readers, tea-leaf diviners, and other such claptrap. To say the least, I was a doubting Thomas.

With all the patience I could muster I listened to glowing tales of this "*ninja* Master's" phenomenal teaching abilities and incredible psychic powers from my young student. For every tale he regaled me with I countered with a logical explanation. But he just would not be dissuaded, for he had found his *swami*, his guru, and he wore black *tabi* (the split-toed *ninja* booties). Muttering under my breath, I agreed to accompany him to the next class Dr. Morris offered, hoping that once I was face-to-face with this *ninja* nut I could talk my student out of wasting his money on this swindler. I had visions of Wayne selling peanut brittle while chanting and wearing saffron robes.

The day of the seminar we traveled to Houston, where my first encounter with Glenn was in the men's rest room. While relieving myself, I observed a tall middle-aged man with a shaven pate enter. Because cops are curious, as well as very paranoid, I watched him out of the corner of my eye. At one point I asked myself if this was the *ninja* con man, though in truth I probably wondered if he was the instructor. A moment later Glenn looked at me and with a trace of a smile said, "Yes, I'm the instructor." Needless to say, he had surprised me by answering my unvoiced question. But within a few minutes I had come up with several reasonable explanations for this act of mental magic.

After an introduction to the scientific side of Glenn's teachings, wherein he explained much of physical effects and theories of meditation, we began our first meditation. I was introduced to a world of Tibetan flaming swords, vortexes of psychic energy, and tiny silver cymbals ringing in my ears. These were only mild preludes to seeing Masaaki Hatsumi, the *soke* of the largest legitimate traditional *ninja* lineage in the world, manifest himself in a smoky green haze over Glenn's sitting body. As for seeing the human body's aura for the first time, that was nothing compared to my encounter with a midnight-black, malevolent-looking infant hovering behind my eyelids. Worse yet, its umbilical cord snaked down to root itself in my third eye. Believe me, for a Presbyterian-raised, hard-core Republican, and closed-minded Southern cop it had been one hell of a long and different day.

Glenn's seminar, and those that followed, opened to me a world I had only read about in texts on ancient religions or in science fiction fantasy novels. In the year and a half to come I would feel Kali's sword slide across my neck as she cradled my head against the hard muscles of her belly. I would enjoy psychic sex with her or other goddesses and would waltz with my feminine self in Damo's Cave. I learned sword skills from *tengu* and fought with demons while the Norse god Loki looked on with a knowing smile. I would hear a multitude of voices whispering in my ear when I failed to follow Glenn's rules for a safe rising of my kundalini energy (thank God they never belonged to Sam, the dog next door).

I experienced the pale moonlight of living in a different world, had periods of wild paranoia, and experienced and suffered strange paranormal events. Things that go bump in the night manifested themselves to liven up both my days and nights. Once I regained some control and cooled off, I was rewarded with out-of-body incidents and was transformed into an owl, a hawk, and a spider. I held hands with angels and stood upon a balcony, looking down on the universe, with something or someone I think may have been a god. I was treated to the vision of a pane of vertical glass through which an angel with Medusa-like tresses erupted. The tips of her undulating hair were topped with tiny faces who sang a heavenly chorale as she ascended up and out of my vision. I feared I might be mad on more than one occasion.

With Glenn's guidance and support I conquered those fears and eventually healed psychological wounds, even some I was unaware of. I felt the loving presence of long-dead relatives and was released by them from foolish guilt for slights and wrongs, real or imagined, done them. Each episode or experience took me toward an experience unlike any I could ever have imagined, the arousal of the kundalini.

That experience was the emotional and spiritual awakening brought about by my dogged determination and Glenn's support and teachings, which culminated one afternoon in January 1997 with a ride on a white-hot serpent who carried me like a rocket to explode ourselves in the most intense golden white light ever imagined. There I was flooded with waves of ecstasy and profound insights. I became the light and the darkness as well. I became everything and realized I was therefore nothing as well.

Glenn's teachings and guidance opened to me the other half of the world of martial arts. His "short path" or "warrior's path" to enlightenment did more for me in two years than the previous twenty-six. The concepts of "true action" and *mushin* (emptiness) are now tangible and within my reach. His methods, explained in *Path Notes of an American Ninja Master* and *Shadow Strategies of an American Ninja Master* are amazingly simple. In easy terms he tells us how to break through, or for some of us to climb over, the complex walls of our mind and open to the powers of self and universe. Goaded on by him, I discovered that enlightenment exists in each and every person's mind. We simply hide it from ourselves behind walls of self-delusion and fear.

Through his autobiographical ramblings, deprecating humor, and convoluted but insightful musings, the good doctor points out a path, a *do*, as the Japanese refer to it. A path to understanding of self and others. *Budo* (war way) may be the "high road," but it's rocky!

The reader of this third book in his esoteric series should realize that while Glenn Morris is an industrial-cum-transpersonal psychologist, he is at heart a martial art genius. His path is the warrior's route to enlightenment and is only for those who are intelligent, strong of heart, and resolute of nature.

I firmly believe that my own kundalini rising was as much from his esoteric training as it was from the martial skills he joyfully pounded into me whenever we found a place I could fall down repeatedly. With decades of *karate, judo, aikido,* and *jujitsu* under my respective black belts and almost twenty years of field-testing those skills as a policeman, when I say Glenn can walk his talk, I know of what I speak. Having your "clock cleaned" with painful ease by Dr. Morris is a wake-up call similar to religious conversion. Today I may not fully understand the concept of *bushi no nasake* (the gentleness of a warrior) but I am much different from the know-it-all tough cop that came to debunk his Houston seminar on meditation techniques for martial artists.

The Japanese value the strength of character necessary to conquer both your enemies and yourself. Often decades, if not entire lifetimes, are spent in the pursuit of the physical and spiritual skills of a master. Those who master both are referred to as *renshi* (a victor in many battles). I have met only a few who are truly *renshi* in the multitude claiming Master status. I place Glenn in the forefront of that small group. When I met him, I had all the pride and vanity that comes with mastery of the physical. I had no idea that there was anything else out there, so with puffed-out chest I surveyed my world, master of everything I saw. With the patience and skill of a real master Glenn became my *sensei*, a term often misinterpreted to mean "teacher." In fact it refers to someone who has walked the path before you—a guide. Glenn became my guide to a wonderful world and a new life as a true human being.

Foreword

I hope you enjoy this book. I encourage you to read *Path Notes* and *Shadow Strategies* for a better understanding of the journey ahead of you. Should you decide to apply the information you'll find within those books, please heed my advice: Follow the rules. Keep your hands and feet inside the vehicle, because friend, you are in for the ride of your life!

Robin Martin, *deshi*
Lake Charles, Louisiana, 1997

Foreword

In the old Norse saga, weird meant your fate, your destiny, your doom. No man could escape his weird, that destiny set for him by the Normans. In time, it came to mean unearthly, and today, odd or strange. Many of these meanings can be applied to what Dr. Morris calls the esoteric and I would call the internal martial arts. Weird in the sense of doom did not mean bad, as it colloquially does today, just as other older meanings are hidden in the liturgical use of *awful* and *dreadful*.[1] This disconnection is not only lexical! The lack of a clear understanding of our Western traditions and of the true internal martial arts of the East means that many of the meanings and explanations for certain types of training are lost to most martial artists today. This discussion was part of my initial conversation with Dr. Glenn Morris over green tea in the back room of a biotech firm's startup laboratory.

Glenn was kind enough to see me, based on the recommendation of a mutual friend, Sellers Smith. Years ago and far away, Sellers and I were training partners, among other things, and started the journey that led him to a fourth *dan* in *ninpo* and Glenn's friendship. It led me to years of study in *shing yi chuan* and later to *savate danse de rue*. (These are on opposite ends of the martial arts spectrum, but I have always been a bit bipolar.) Sellers, who was mentioned in Glenn's first book, and I remained close, so he was kind enough to introduce me to a new playmate. What followed was the growth of a friendship based on a shared interest in combative techniques (no sporting stuff allowed), the internal or esoteric arts, lots of tea and good food, and, as the goddess (my wife) says, "equally defective senses of humor." That first day was fascinating. Glenn's approach was different from anything I had seen before. I was no stranger to the internal arts and was surprised to see Glenn's power was of the same order as Sifu Kenny Gong's senior students!

Sifu Kenny Gong and his student Tom Morrissey are one pole of my martial art world and the other is *savate* as taught by Professor Buitron. *Shing yi chuan,* as taught by Sifu Gong, taught Westerners the techniques that cultivated internal power. Tom is my teacher and in many ways my big brother. I was originally introduced to the martial arts via judo by my father, who practiced Chinese *karate* and white lotus *kung fu* back before it all became popular. Over the years I studied a range of arts, earned a black belt or two, and most important had my head handed to me by a chain-smoking pot-bellied Chinese restaurant owner in his parking lot. (He said, "So you do *karate?* I do *kung fu.* Want to play?" Being a young seventeen, I said sure. Bad move. The lesson is, don't play with old out-of-shape people who invite you to. Age and treachery really do win.) This started me down the path of the internal arts. Then while at R.P.I. in Troy New York, I met Tom Morrissey, who had just started teaching Gong-style *shing yi chuan.* I was home. Tom and I kept in touch after I got a "real" job and he continued training me, sometimes long distance. In the meantime, at Tom's advice, I studied other arts for technique and people to practice on. I met some great teachers in *aikido, arnis, isshinryu karate, kung fu,* and less common arts like *kenjitsu, gatka, pai lum, ninpo,* and *hung gar.*[2] *Shing yi chuan* remained my first love, as its principles seemed to underlie the other arts, and no one else talked as clearly of the internal as did Kenny Gong. When I heard of Sifu Gong's death, it was like the death of my own grandfather. I think we all mourn him still. May perpetual light shine upon his spirit and may his memory be eternal.

Several years later, I met the other pole of my martial arts life, Professor Paul-Raymond Buitron III, who is the *only* teacher of the full system of *savate* (also called *savate danse de rue*) outside of France. Professor "Popeye" Buitron teaches the surviving Western combat system, which he was instrumental in preserving and refining.

He is the first American to earn his silver glove in France, the first American certified to teach *savate-boxe Française,* the ranking *savateur* in North America, and the person most responsible for saving the combat system of *savate* from total degradation into a sport. Of his generation of *savateurs,* he was the only one willing to listen, to seek out the old maitres and codify the street techniques into a teachable form. A fine and honorable man, he is both a kindred spirit and friend. Interestingly, *savate danse de rue* has no esoteric teachings at all, although the combative logic it teaches may be unmatched in the martial arts. No other system develops fighters as quickly, nor does any look as graceful, in my opinion. Professor Buitron once described it as "as beautiful as ballet and as brutal as a dog fight." This is very true. I was home in another way, having found, in the words of Count de Baruzy, that "*savate* was at once life, death, and resurrection."

I was quite happily settled in Texas when Sellers introduced Glenn to me by e-mail. Since we were both in Houston, I dropped by for tea. That first day Glenn helped me understand some things about the movement of *chi* I had missed and cleared some blocks that opened my energy even more. He is the first person outside of the *shing yi chuan* system I have met with this level of power (it's huge), and he is a great teacher with a real gift at pulling things together across cultures. Despite all the talk and the present surge of books on the subject, people who really know something about the internal are few and far between. Very few players have appreciable power. Most New Agers talk about it but lack any experience. Some claim to have learned from the Chinese but haven't done their homework.

Since the training you do affects how your energy looks, even those who know a bit about postures and movement may still not realize what just walked in energywise. Glenn says that *hoshineers* have auras that look like a psychopaths, while *shing yi* players look almost normal, except they burn way too bright.[3] The latter may be true, as some stories exist about people feeling a *shing yi* player's energy and being shocked when it expanded to repel them when they poked it. Tom described this power as being like a furnace, contained and blazing. Most people have very thin, light auras. Beginning meditators are surrounded by more light, *chi kung* practitioners glow, while masters radiate, and under certain conditions look hallowed.

As we all share the same biochemistry and physiology, one would expect certain concepts to be similar across cultures. If you don't believe this, read Renaissance English swordmaster George Silver's description of the twofold mind along with an authoritative book on Zen in the Japanese or Ch'an in the Chinese martial arts.[4] The external approach may simply depend on a teacher's outlook and his or her tradition—what Hatsumi-soke calls "local differences."

Glenn's approach is very metaphysical, while mine is not. Glenn teaches his students to see auras, work with energy, massage *chi*, and other topics not normally considered to be part of a martial art. I spent time sparring with him with my eyes closed, letting him punch at the back of my head, fencing rapier or *la canne* against his *katana*, trying *savate danse de rue* against his style, and generally terrorizing the bystanders. He made me learn how to undo some of the damage we cause and how to repair a damaged green belt. While there are lots of wonderfully nasty tricks in the *hoshinroshiryu* system, there is also, in the upper ranks, an emphasis on healing. The theory seems to be that if you break one of the *kyu* ranks, you should also be able to fix one, or at least stabilize them for the real healers. Thankfully, you are not required to.

Glenn's ability to present the cross-cultural core of something makes it easier to understand. He has taken many of his students though the kundalini experience. Thankfully, unlike with Robin Martin and others, none of that weird stuff happened to me. *Shing yi chuan* is a gentle, slow approach to developing internal power compared to *hoshinroshiryu's* interesting full-speed-ahead-guns-blazing approach.[5] I had spent years doing its breathing and *chi kung* exercises. Glenn helped me in fully opening the orbits and taught me all sorts of interesting things that worked, but I never had the fireworks. A bit of fogginess when the head centers opened, a bit of sleepiness, but no strangeness, no visions, and no *chi* sickness. I don't feel particularly deprived about missing any of it, either. If my experience is the result of a slower path, that's fine with me as I have no urge to court insanity. (My wife/goddess says I am unstable enough as it is. I still think it is all *prelest*, especially the nubile young maidens of blue hue that some people describe.[6] If you ignore them they go away.)

Glenn also teaches lots of fun things to do to your friends. It probably distressed his relatively stuffy corporate neighbors to see two Ph.Ds in suits hacking at either other with various sharp things in the atrium, but it really is too hot outside in a Houston summer to play on the lawn. Anyhow, no one ever complained. A lot of the stuff in the internal arts seems easier to learn as part of a martial system, probably due to almost instantaneous feedback.

He doesn't claim to be an enlightened guru and dislikes the concept of *deshi*, as it means you aren't thinking for yourself. Not thinking means you aren't trying new things and bringing them back into the *ryu*. That means you are probably boring. A major surprise to me was that several of the students mentioned in his books follow my faith. Maybe Eastern Christianity is more tolerant of the internal arts than the people at Hillsdale College, who wanted to burn him at the stake. Maybe we feel an obligation to try the more difficult cases. Anyway, the differences seem to work out to the good, although I still burn candles for his soul.

This book has some exercises and techniques using subtle energy that are nice, but the important parts are the traps and delusions for the martial artist. Regardless of how good you are, you are never unbeatable and there are always limits. G. K. Chesterton said that the error of stoicism is the belief you can always do what you can sometimes do. *Shidoshi* Ed Sones was blunter: "No one gets out unscathed." Tom Morrissey warned, "Sometimes you get hurt to end it fast." Sifu Kenny Gong said, "My favorite technique is to run away. It is very hard to stop a shotgun." My father still asks if I can block a bullet yet. (I think the implied question is, are you stupid enough to try?)

However, the minute someone starts teaching the internal arts, be it in *tai chi, chi gong, pa kua,* or *ninjitsu*, common sense appears to vanish. Con artists come out of the woodwork. *Ninpo* refers to *genjutsu,* the skills of illusion and deceit. Sifu John Painter ran a whole series of articles in *Internal Arts Magazine* about how martial art *chi* tricks work, and "Dr." Lueng Ting even published two rather strange books on *Secrets of the Vagabonds* (the old tricks used in China to fool the gullible). In the Western tradition, there are collections of similar tricks that seem to imply incredible skills or power, like *Sword Feats* (from the 1700s), *Secrets of the Strong Man* (1940s carnival tricks to show abnormal power), and an incredibly large literature of mental and physical magic tricks. The line between real *chi* and trickery can be hard to see. Through the years I must have seen or bought or read thirty books on developing the power of your *chi.* Maybe two had authors who knew what they were doing. No one mentioned that for most people it can take years, and for some it's impossible. As Sifu Gong would say, "you show."

Even worse are the mind games you get into if you start believing a false teacher. They will offer to teach you the only true martial art, how to be a human death machine, or how to become a secret master, but only as long as you pay and promise absolute obedience. The current fascination with tantric sex is a good example. If it really is a secret art, how did all these people learn it? How many charlatans taught *karate* in the sixties, *kung fu* in the seventies, *ninpo* in the eighties, and probably are claiming to teach *pentak silat* today? Most of this fake stuff is actually pretty easy to check out. This book will help; Glenn doesn't pull any punches here and the money and pain you save will be your own.

Enjoy the walking meditation. Watch out for invisible green dragons, large spiders, friendly old bears, blue nubiles, and white tigers. They will all go away if you ignore them. Think of Glenn's world as a visit to a national park where you aren't allowed to feed the inhabitants. If you must interact with them through gaucheness or curiosity, remember they think of you as food. Be polite. Glenn will take you to all sorts of weird and wonderful places.

Kevin "Armado" Menard,
Denton, Texas, 1998

Notes

1. Meaning to fill one with awe and inspiring fear or dread, neither of which has to be bad.

2. *Gatka* is the sword-fighting system of the Sikhs, which in the United States seems to be mainly studied by incredibly strong-spirited women. It is hard to find a teacher as they are relatively rare and often unwilling to teach the unreferred. The art is one of the few that openly cultivates the kundalini and the energy body. Certain exercises are even done to strengthen and extend the aura.

3. "Hoshineers" is a Robin Martin word for one who practices the internal arts of the *hoshinroshiryu*.

4. George Silver was a seventeenth-century English Master of Defense who wrote *Paradoxes of Defense* and *Brief Instructions in Defense*. He discusses mind set and attitude in combat.

5. Interesting doesn't always mean good. Read the science fiction book by Pratchett, *Interesting Times,* or ponder the Cantonese curse, "May you have an interesting life."

6. *Prelest* means delusion or misdirection. Read large parts of the *Philokalia* or the writings of Theoplan the Recluse or Ignatius Brianchaninov. All have descriptions, some of which seem similar to practices from Glenn's first and second books.

Acknowledgments

This book is for Aree, without whose support I could not have done this sort of thing, and for Sara Glenn Mariko, who will probably never appreciate how much she has taught me. It is for Masaaki Hatsumi-soke, who continues to allow me to peek into his art with wonder, and it is for all the *ninja* and *ninja* wanna-bes who have offered me friendship and training opportunities over the years. It is for practitioners of other martial arts both East and West, and scholars of the healing and esoteric arts. It is for the martial masters and members of the World Head of Family and Sokeship Council, whose questions and answers have kindled my burning curiosity. May I continue to learn from you, and in the spirit of *giri* (enormous debt) offer up another book of *ura* (inner) techniques and commentary.

CHAPTER ONE

Introduction to Esoteric Budo

The source of Budo is God's lover, the spirit of loving protection for all beings. True Budo is to accept the spirit of the universe, to keep the peace of the world, and to correctly produce, protect, and cultivate all beings in nature.

—Morihei Ueshiba, founder of *aikido*, friend of Takamatsu-sensei

There is no prejudice so strong as that which arises from a fancied exemption from all prejudice.

—William Hazlitt, essayist, *On the Tendency of Sects,* 1817

Whatever crushes individuality is despotism, by whatever name it may be called.

—John Stuart Mill, thinker, *On Liberty,* 1859

True *budo* has to do with living well under all conditions. The viewpoint of the strategist leads one to consider the esoteric as an area of life that extends into death. As death of the body is a given, a person concerned with spiritual life will be curious about techniques that extend longevity before death and may even preserve immortality after death. I write about the martial arts from the perspective of a transpersonal psychologist—a teacher of meditation, *jujutsu,* and *chi kung;* and an occasional and personal student who practices *ninjutsu* under Masaaki Hatsumi-soke of *bujinkan budo taijutsu* or the *bujinden*—and in this book I will use examples drawn primarily from those arts, though I have, and do, study others. My viewpoint is not always shared by my confederates. I warn you now that some consider my opinions and behavior controversial.

I like to use a martial or strategic viewpoint when I think about things as it forces me to address the consequences of action. The strategist is more pragmatic than the dreamer because the positive is not always possible. When one looks at one's life objectively it can often be seen as a series of decision-trees. Some trees do better than others, depending on the terrain. The first job I ever fancied as a child was that of forest ranger, but I never could master the math that rendered a tree into board feet, so I followed after my professional soldier cousin into the army. When my hitch was over I took my GI Bill and eventually became a professor of communication and social psychology, and a leadership consultant to rust belt heavy industry. My martial hobbies and *ronin* experiences increased my value to those who hired me (See *Path Notes of an American Ninja Master* and *Shadow Strategies of an American Ninja Master*).

In this book I will address issues that affect both the religious and martial practitioner of meditation and some aspects of shamanism/alchemy, as practiced both in the East and the West, that may be used by a practitioner of *budo*. Three chapters are devoted to the trait analysis of "martial arts madness," a general term I first heard used by Hatsumi-soke that applies to a group of maladies seldom discussed in clinical journals, because individuals bearing the symptoms are seldom seen by psychiatrists but do occasionally lock horns with the military or police. Energy techniques, meditation, and *chi*-sickness will be discussed throughout the text, with more of an emphasis on Western traditions than in my previous two books. Of course, transpersonal commentary and strategies for getting through life with minimal soul damage will be discussed. There will also be tales submitted by interested parties. I'm sure *chi*-sickness is a factor that those in the know probably wish to avoid. I'm not really certain it can be avoided by the short-path practitioner, but the descriptions I've collected for the chapter on *chi*-sickness may make those who have had or are having similar experiences happy. Misery loves company, and often the sharing of symptoms (particularly the survival of said symptoms) is cheering to the neophyte. *Chi*-sickness will be discussed in terms of physical symptoms by some of my students and some verifiable and credible *ninpo* practitioners in Chapter Eleven.

You may study various forms of meditation for years and derive nothing worth writing home about, or you may luck out, find someone who actually knows something, and make interesting changes in amazingly short periods of time. In this book I'll expose some exercises used in *hoshintao chi kung* as developed by certified teachers of the system. When you want more, or want more personalized help, it is easier to attend seminars than to go on a quest. This, the last book in this series, is a collection of short essays dealing with the psychological and transpersonal aspects of the practice of *budo*. It pops some spiritual balloons and makes the identifying of the wackos a little easier for the neophyte.

Most of the stories in this book were chosen to illustrate some aspect of the kundalini experience, and the reader may note that some aspects are not particularly in tune with our times. However, the Goddesses' riddles are critical to following evolutionary purpose, and solving these riddles can save your life. Many of the stories, whether written by a master or an innocent, contain a description of one of the *siddhi*, or its perversion. The writers are not the usual knuckle-draggers who give bad or self-serving advice around the art they teach, but the students and hobbyists who for the most part have better things to do with their lives than pound their chests and bash each other about. If you can keep your inner biker-mama's left hand off the throttle, their powers of observation may take you to a new place in your development. The martial artist is often faced with the tyrannical incorporation of what significant others think we should be, as well as the discrepancy between our actual selves and the self-perception of the unobtainable ideal.

Some of these vignettes are great riddles and will have you scratching your head but not levitating. I have doctored a few in terms of spelling, word choice, and grammar; my old editor should be rewarded for all the good things she beat into me, teaching me to write while she was saving trees, sailing yachts, and living well. (As I made a change, it was usually with the thought that this will make Kathy Glass laugh out loud. Now Mike Shaeffer has the editorial responsibility of keeping me in shallow water. Remember their names. You might want to do a book some day without revealing too much folly.)

Some of the stories deal with medical aspects, some with strategy, some with teaching styles, some with personalities, and some with real magic, magick, and lots of madness. You too may find yourself maddened by what they wrote, but in every case, there was a semblance to my own experience. As you read, see how easily they reveal their secrets to the knowing, yet with little traps for the uninitiated. If you aren't on the way north by the time you have finished with this book you will have to learn Chinese, Tibetan, Hindi, Aramaic, Middle German, and perhaps Japanese. You are too hard for me and need a crueler teacher's hand to force your proper movement.

There was a lot of good material sent in with the tripe. The stories in this book are the most fun of those I cared to risk associating with my name. It is difficult enough that I have to put up with assertive ignoramuses, but as a psychologist one mustn't ignore the standards of the scientific community as well. Double-edged indeed, this oathless society. Some critics have claimed I make it too easy for my readers and should quit spoon-feeding the ignorant as they won't value the gift, but every heaven hath its hell in aging. Alzheimer's is a not-too-distant family legacy of the body outliving the abstract functions of the brain. I try to be succinct, since I never know when the last connected thought will fade into the encroaching night, strangled by genetic assassins so silently that it is never missed by the fixed stare into the past where she and I were happy. Oh, sweet, sweet senility!

It is a wonder and a miracle to me that I am not in jail over one or the other. My mother, a brilliant and honest woman, said when visiting my professorial domain a long time before her mind went and after my father's rude mental departure, "This is very hard for me to grasp, as I still see the little boy I had to spank. It is strange to me that you are the most ethical of all my sons." (It was a good day with lots of students saying, "Hello, Dr. Morris," and people treating me with respect as I showed her around the pleasant college campus and my big office and personal library at the Leadership Development Center.) She was as surprised saying this as I was hearing it. So take that familial sharing as a paltry indicator, yet unsupported figment, of a suspected willingness to hand you a ladder of light at some point in the dark. If I remember. *Buyu ikkan.*

Esoteric Martial Arts as a Way of Life and Death

Many Americans want martial arts masters to fit the mold of the altruistic religious master or saint. As much as this ideal might improve the position of martial artists in terms of social acceptance, the reality falls somewhere between fat bleeping chance and nada. The eight concepts concerning behavior to be practiced in *budo* are listed on page 30 of *Shadow Strategies*. The religious models that come closest to *budo* in terms of turning out Buddhas might be the monks of Zen, the crazy wisdom practitioners of Tibet, the tantrics of India, the sufis of Islam, and the knight-errants of Christianity. These models have created a mythology of behavior that probably won't live up to the reality of in-your-face objectivity and sense of humor that exists in upper-level martial arts.

Immortality has a variety of meanings in English, just as *chi* has a variety of meanings in Chinese. Expecting your local martial arts master to be your spiritual guru is probably putting a lot of responsibility and karmic debt on the wrong person. There are a few "*budo*men" who are actually Buddhamen, but they are few and far between in the Asian arts, which might indicate to the astute that the Western equivalent is even harder to locate. I have met four who can be considered touched by God: two, as priests, fail out of arrogance, and the other two deny it, though they glow in the dark to me. For the most part, *budo*men, if they live long enough, realize their state is the natural way of being or living in the face of death as a human being. And because the enlightened state is the way we are supposed to be, there is very little that is special about it except its rarity. There is no conversion, only evolution. Study on this until you absorb in toto.

Martial Traditions, Ancient and Modern, in the West

Many Asian and particularly American stylists are unaware that Europe has as long and as developed a martial history as the Orient. In the following pages, I am going to review the history of the Western arts and discuss a bit about *savate* as a combative art, because I see in *savate,* particularly its combatics, a history similar to some of the schools of *jujitsu* and *ninjutsu*.

The European unarmed arts can be traced to the Greeks' boxing, wrestling, and *pankraton. Pankraton* means "all-powers fighting," and was a system that used the whole body in combat. It was played in the Olympics and taught in Greek and later Roman gymnasiums to all classes. Both literary and pictorial descriptions of techniques have survived. The Roman legions were trained in this and in *cesta* (loaded or spiked fist). The Roman Empire spread it across Europe, the Middle East, and North Africa. Written references to the techniques, the training, and its generality are found in literature up to the fourth century. After this, it is reported in military manuals up to the fall of the Holy Roman Empire to the Turks in the 1450s.

In Anglo-Saxon England the sword of the warrior was held in the same regard as the sword of the samurai. Arthur's sword Excalibur, the most well-known example, was said to be wielded by Richard the Lionhearted in the Crusades (a story with high wader probability). The surviving technology and archaeological record of sword development and training techniques in the West were matched and quickly subsumed by the cleverness of the firearms and explosives industries, pressured to perform by centuries of religious and expeditious warfare. The War of the Roses and The Hundred Years War were part of a history so horrid that some who fled to America still do not wear buttons out of fear of being thought military or conscriptable.

Circa 1410, the oldest surviving arms manual, *Il Flors Duellatorum,* was published in Italy. This title represents the start of a recorded history of training manuals and a documented history of "sword schools." Like the Eastern sword systems, the European schools taught a wide range of weapons as well as unarmed techniques. *Talhoffers Fechtbuch* (1467) shows techniques still used in *savate danse de rue* today. As printing presses were not yet around, these manuals were made at great cost for the students and friends of the author. They should be considered to be closer to the secret scrolls of some Eastern systems than publicly issued books. (Interested parties should consult Clements' book on rapier and cut/thrust swords, *Renaissance Swordsmanship,* or the Hammervatz Forum for intelligent discussions of the combat fencing systems of Europe.) Along with the weapons, Renaissance students were also taught "all manner of grips, kicking, wrestling, and strikes," to quote George Silver, an Elizabethan Master of Arms. If you can read Middle English, you will enjoy Master Silver's pointed humor and cutting insights.

German wrestling manuals have also survived from the 1500s and show techniques that are brutal beyond modern standards. Many of the woodcuts show techniques that are identical to those pictured in early books on *savate*. *Savate* as a separate fighting art is first mentioned in the mid-1600s in a poem.

An even older form of *savate* developed from the fighting styles used in northern France. It came from a variety of sources, including *chausson*, English wrestling, and boxing. Originally it was a kicking style that used open-hand techniques; later, punches were added due to experience in the ring. This sport is called *boxe-Française*. *Savate* was first formalized in the early 1800s as a set of fifteen leg and fifteen cane techniques. Later, more kicks were added, as well as the hand techniques. The style was first associated with thugs and criminals, to the point that a *savateur* was consider a brutal savage. Later it became popular with the military and police, resulting in greater social acceptance.

The popularity of *savate's* second discipline, *la canne* (the cane), grew among the nobility under the Napoleons as they introduced techniques from the short sword into the system. As France had very close relations with Spain in this period, the influence of the Spanish sword schools can be seen in *la canne* and *baton* (short staff or *jo*). Spain and Portugal conquered most of the Western world, including the Americas, with mostly cut-and-thrust weaponry and single-shot muskets and cannon.

In the 1800s, interestingly, the French government's approach to treating a street fight as a potential recruitment drive for the Foreign Legion (i.e., go to jail or join the valiant struggle against the Moroccan *tauregs* as a private with a funny hat and new name) assisted the development of *lutte parisienne*. This style of grappling developed techniques to conceal the attack and make the incident look like an accident (similar to high-level *ninjutsu* and basic *hoshinjutsu*).

Panache (use of clothing) was also popularized in this period as a method of gaining an advantage in a fight so it could be quickly won. *Panache* may be the least well-defined discipline; it is sometimes called "the secret in the bottle" and comes directly from the old combative sword schools. *Panache* appears to have esoteric meanings similar to attitude and energy when the term is discussed with some of the older players. It is rumored that one of the masters of *panache* enjoyed loitering in the subways of Paris in his latter years as an exercise in street cleaning and waste control. His litter from the wee hours would be deposited in tidy piles for the flics to collect in the morning. On some strange point of Napoleonic law he was neither pursued nor encouraged. The police probably regarded his vigilante hobby as noblesse oblige and secretly admired his tactics.

The Western fighting and grappling arts survived to the early 1900s, when the influence of sportsmen changed them from local fighting styles, like Lancaster, Cornish, and Derby wrestling (all of which permitted kicking) or fisticuffs (boxing that allowed kicks and holds) into the sanitized rule-encumbered (no biting or gouging) versions used today.

The original difference between boxing, wrestling, and *savate* was one of focus: boxing, for example, concentrated on hitting but allowed other techniques. Only in this century did it become exclusively a sport of punching. Wrestling has only been cleaned up in the last century. Seldom written about, but true, is that Abraham Lincoln often performed feats of strength and wrestled no-holds-barred for purses. In one bout he used a bit of doggy-do to subdue an opponent.

More information on the history of Western martial arts, with particular emphasis on *savate,* can be found in Paul. R. Buitron's *Encyclopedia of Savate Danse de Rue.* (See the Bibliography for more information on this limited edition book. Today *savate danse de rue* (at least in Dallas and Laredo, Texas) teaches the four disciplines of *boxe-Francaise* (foot-fighting), *la canne et baton* [the weapon system including *la canne, baton, couteau, fouette, and rasoir*], *lutte parisienne* (grappling), and *panache* (use of environmental objects). *Savate danse de rue* was developed by Professor Buitron as a means of saving the older techniques of *savate.* With the encouragement of *Grande-Maitre* Robert Paturel and *Maitre* Jean-Paul Viviani, he developed a program to teach the entire system of *savate. Danse de rue* retains the sporting aspects of *boxe-Francaise* and *la canne de combat* but recovers the combat skills lost in the sporting forms.

Boxe-Francaise has been mellowed into a pure sport form similar to *tae kwan do,* and certain sporting practitioners look down upon the combat players from a stance of specious moral superiority akin to *aikidoists* regarding *jujutsuka.* (When I became aware of Professeur Buitron's struggle to preserve and formalize the combatics in *savate,* I was intrigued, as I had a similar struggle with *hoshin* years before. It led to our developing a long-distance friendship. Banging heads with our dual student Dr. Kevin Menard allowed me to experience the quality of his work.)

A *savateur* is ranked by gloves for technical ability starting with blue, then green, red (*shodan* equivalent), white, yellow, and finally silver. In addition, a separate teaching ladder exists of coach, initiateur, aide-moniteur, moniteur, and professeur. While certain levels of technical skill are required to attain teaching rank, both specialized training and testing are also needed. This means that some silver gloves are not allowed to teach despite their technical skill. A teacher of any grade is considered a disciple, not a student. Moniteurs and above are called "donnors," meaning they give back to the art. Silver glove is only awarded to those eighteen years of age or older. Youngsters are given a violet glove and test for silver on becoming eighteen. In the sport of *boxe-Francaise,* a bronze glove can be earned in place of the white and yellow gloves in competition.

Now you know a little bit about a Western tradition that is in some ways very similar to the Japanese *bujinkan* traditions concerning the three schools of *ninpo.* For the most part, Western traditions have been forgotten with the advent of rifles, pistols, and other fun things that shoot fast and explode from a distance, but warriors will always find ways to seek advantage, whether armed or not.

Esoteric and Religious Traditions

Gnosticism, Hesychasm, Hermeticism, Kaballah, Wicca, the rituals of the Golden Dawn Society, and the various pagan ways are all pure Western or Middle Eastern-derived paths of esoteric development (I don't intentionally exclude Native American traditions from this list, I just don't know their names or enough about them). Each contains exoteric and esoteric teachings, and if one can get past the rituals and codes of the external presentation to the hidden practices concerning the training of intention, meditation, and breath techniques for awakening the inner fire, there are marked similarities in what is described. Most of these systems also include warnings concerning improper indulgence in techniques leading to paranormal events, superhuman strength, and insanity.

In Russia the practice of Hesychasm (derived from the Greek for a "quiet breath of life") was restricted to monastics by the Orthodox church to reduce the number of fruitcakes running naked through the woods, snow, and streets, importuning relative strangers with ecstatic tales of their visions. You might recall Rasputin's effect on the last Romanov Tsar. The Orthodox churches have preserved a collection of writings on prayer wherein various methods are discussed as leading to *prelest* (delusion) and insanity. Many of the practices I have described in the first two books of this series fall into this blacklist for the church as they lead to enhanced powers rather than to a vision of God (if you seek a supreme way of being, you may find something to your liking in *budo*). However, the warrior's path is not the monk's path. For most practitioners of *budo* there are usually no skilled abbots to send you back to your room when things get too strange.

CHAPTER TWO

Breath, Intent, and Energy: Occult Practice, East and West

Die Religionen mussen alle toleriert werden ... denn hier muss ein jeder nach seiner Fasson selig werden (All religions must be tolerated ... every man must go to heaven in his own way).

—Frederick the Great, emperor, 1740

It does me no harm for my neighbor to say there are twenty gods, or no God. It neither picks my pocket or breaks my leg.

—Thomas Jefferson, planter, architect, and successful revolutionary, *Notes on the State of Virginia,* 1782

No unwritten law has ever been more binding than unwritten custom supported by popular opinion.

—Carrie Chapman Catt, expert witness, U.S. Senate hearing, 1900

Esoterica and Occult

Esoterica exists in most popular religions as part of their core element of mysticism. In modern times this is poorly understood by the majority of the followers of any given religion. The outer *(omote)* or exoteric form of religious observance is generally so oversimplified or dumbed-down that special training is necessary for those few who seek to understand the inner *(ura)* or esoteric truths that are hidden. Some maintain there is nothing to seek. The esoteric in religion is often regarded as "dangerous knowledge," "cult quackery," or the secret treasures of the power elite ("Who knows what evil lurks in the hearts of men?"). Since I'm a failed Methodist and actually hold the rank of lieutenant colonel in the Chaplain's Corps, I will use Christian illustrations, because poking fun or just simply pointing can be revenged in other less-forgiving religions, though I can say from personal experience that poking fun at Christians is not the safest of pastimes.

Some religious scholars maintain that esoteric Christianity grew out of the influence of the Greek mystery schools. According to these theologians, the universal essence of Jesus' teachings to all is simple: "Abide in me and I in you." This primordial Protestant tendency was overshadowed by what Origen, the third-century Egyptian theologian, spoke of as "the popular irrational faith rather than the special knowledge which leads to a spiritual Christianity." For the most part the spiritual emphasis in Christian ritual has belonged to the churches Orthodox in the ancient forms, or suffered a strange rejuvenation in the fundamental sects. It is easy to see why esoteric statements such as, "You are God" could be misunderstood by the average person and might lead to problems of psychological inflation. Even the safer and male chauvinistic "son of God" has grandiose implications to the true believer. To quote Carl J. Jung, "All esoteric teachings are seeking to grasp that which is unfolding in the psyche without which it is impossible to have any insight." Insight requires understanding, and understanding is best derived from perceptive experience.

Esoteric training aims to reawaken our spiritual awareness naturally through self-discipline, inner work, and outer action. To insist on rigid hierarchies of levels of humanity is a distortion of esotericism as misguided as the sects that proclaim their own way as the ultimate rightness while denying others validity. An overprotective attitude on the part of initiates is also a dangerous thing, therefore esoteric teachings are often reserved for the asking but should not be withheld arbitrarily.

Occultism is concerned with the moral, intellectual, and spiritual evolution of humanity. Occultism is the synthesis of science, mysticism, psychology, philosophy, and religion. It accepts the proven assertions and rejects the untenable assertions requiring faith, dogma, and superstition. The occult is simply a recognition of hidden powers, and the goal of practical occultism is an expansion of consciousness. For most practitioners it is an obsession with the mysteries of human existence. Since the effects are subtle, as the gods move in "mysterious ways," there will always be frauds who claim more knowledge than they actually have. Many of the mysteries are ancient and many of the practices have little use in the modern world.

Many of Jesus' parables have an esoteric or occult meaning. One of the easiest to see is the story of the prodigal son (Luke 15, 11–32), which represents the descent into the material world and the resulting forgetfulness of the divine spark within. When the son (spark) returns to the family he is greeted with rejoicing. This descent and eventual return of the soul from flesh is also a metaphor in the *Song of the Pearl* in the apocryphal *Acts of Thomas*.

All that is stated above for religion is also true for the martial arts. The martial arts have a long history of esoterica, particularly from the Eastern traditions, but in the West as well we have the legends surrounding chivalry and occasional tales of warriors with strange powers on their side or among the most evil of the vanquished. Cut off their heads. Drive stakes through their bodies, or draw and quarter them. Give their souls no rest. Mutilate them. Do not bury them in sacred ground. Leave no trace to comfort their families. . . . With that sort of prejudice about, it is difficult to establish an ecumenical sharing of information. In these more enlightened times we are more likely to poke fun at, rather than holes in, those we do not understand.

Energy

About a hundred years ago the more seminal thinkers in Western physics and psychology began to question the reality of regarding the universe in terms of substance and material, since the paradigms useful for explaining reality were hitting dead ends. Process and system orientations began to be discussed as part of phenomena to be inspected as well as a way to inspect. Energy and thermodynamics became topics open to almost mystical interpretation, and physicists in the last twenty years have begun to confabulate books with titles like the *Tao of Physics* or *The Living Universe* without being stoned in the marketplace or driven from their faculty positions.

In China, in a wide range of disciplines for approximately four thousand years, the scientific regard for or study of living energy has been institutionalized among the Taoist sages (read natural scientists) as *chi* (subtle energy). Taoist sages were generalists of an ilk rarely seen in Western art or academics. These men and women were acknowledged experts in meditation, philosophy, medicine, geomancy, history, mathematics, astronomy, astrology, literature, poetry, scripture, painting, music, liturgy, martial arts, and sorcery. The Taoist prized the attitude of humility and considered self-importance as a temptation resulting in the failure to transcend identity. The greatest Taoists did not care for rank, labels, or status and avoided religious persecution through the development of "the art of invisibility" or subtle movement. Some were obviously the equivalent of the Renaissance folk who dominated Western art and science during the fifteenth and sixteenth centuries in Europe.

Where we in the West emphasized the easily measurable particle side of the Heisenberg equations, the Chinese have investigated the ineffable wave for centuries. Much of what they have said has only been translated recently, and a great deal of what is discussed in these translations is being verified by Western scientists who are able to step out of their own particular discipline's model of reality to experience something that is new to them but ancient in the East. It is ancient but hardly common knowledge. How many quantum physicists do you know?

The Taoist Chinese defined eight forms of *chi*, three of which are common to all human beings; all are accessible to some extent to the determined *chi kung* practitioner. Katchmer has a good explanation of the workings of the Eastern methodologies and perspectives, with enough concrete Western examples, to keep one scratching one's head for quite awhile (see the Bibliography). In this book I will try to provide theory and exercises concerning the use of *chi* from a warrior's as well as a Western phenomenological and transpersonal perspective.

Subtle energy (also called *prana*) can be simply defined materially as living biomagnetics, bioenergetics, or as informational fields resulting from transcendent states based in a common underlying neurobiochemical involvement of biogenic amine temporal lobe interactions, causing an increased interhemispheric integration of the whole brain, resulting in greater synchronization, coherence, and a synthesis of thought and emotion. Subtle energy manifests in high-voltage slow-wave EEG activity originating in the hippocampal-septal area and imposes a synchronous slow-wave pattern on the frontal lobes. Control of subtle energy is usually associated with right-hemisphere dominance, cortical synchronization, and a dominant parasympathetic state. (How's that for substantive hairsplitting?)

There are many psychophysiological procedures that increase the ability to both feel and produce subtle energy. Short-term experiences can be had by ingesting hallucinogens or via activities that produce endogenous opiates, such as distance running or extended motor behavior. A lengthier experience can be induced by fasting, sleep loss, thirst, or auditory stimulation. Intense sensory stimulation such as physical torture and temperature extremes, as well as lucid-dreaming sleep states, community rituals, and meditation can be invaluable training aids for the seeker. Natural psychic "powers" can also be derived from a variety of psychophysiological imbalances or sensitivities resulting from hereditarily transmitted nervous system liabilities or enhancements, depending on the reliability of control. Also, epileptic-like states resulting from injury, disease, or other trauma to the central nervous system, temporal lobes, hippocampal-septal system, and amygdala are documented. One can take one's choice of vehicles. I recommend using a risk/damage rating of procedures and possible outcomes to select what may work for you.

Meditation seems a clear winner over torture, fasting, thirst, and sleep loss; however, Hispanic-Indio flagellants seem to derive some sort of psychic benefit from fasting, whipping themselves, and carrying crosses up and down mountains during inclement weather. The Cheyenne and Sioux warriors used to hang themselves from a pole with ropes driven through their pectoral muscles and their feet barely touching the ground. They danced in pain until the ropes pulled through or the dancer collapsed, resulting in a rush of endocrine activity. The practice was ritualized as the Sun Dance, and participants were often granted visions. Sufi learn to dance to an inner music. Sitting erect and breathing deeply while looking within may be a slower way to find the light in the inner dark, but the scars are not visible, except to a seer. Some of the Hindu tantric practitioners state boldly that those who speak of a kundalini arousal without pain, fear, and experience of hell are only experiencing the milder forms of *kriya* arousal and are guilty of the sin of self-importance. They have not touched the stone; they would just like you to believe they have.

Breath

A Chou Dynasty (500 B.C.E.) inscription on breathing can be translated, "When transforming the breath, the inhalation must be full to gather the magic. To gather the magic, fullness must be extended. When it is extended it can penetrate downward. When it can penetrate downward, it is magic. When it descends it becomes calm, solidifies, and is both strong and firm. When it is strong and firm, it will germinate. If it germinates it will grow and retreat upward. If it is attracted back, then a man can reach both heaven and earth in the same breath. When it retreats upward, it reaches the top of the head. When it falls forward, it can caress the feet and still press down. The secret powers of Providence move above. The secret powers of the Earth move below. He who follows this will live; he who acts against this will die."

This "force" or the effects of refining the breath go under different names in different countries where different systems of meditation developed to make human beings more human. *Prana* (Sanskrit), *ki* (Japanese), *pneuma* (Greek), *ruah* (Hebrew), *ruh* (Arabic), *chi* (Chinese), and *orgone* (Native American) are all names for the same phenomena that only recently has begun to be accepted in Western allopathic medicine as *subtle energy* (English). Just this year a famous cardiologist remarked that all disease begins as an imbalance of energy. Wow, how insightful.

The "embryonic breath," "baby breath," or "Buddha breath" is couched in religious, mystical, and esoteric symbolism, but the practice as used by martial artists is more a series of physical exercises than dogma or doctrine. The practitioner opens the bottom of his or her lungs by moving the intestines down while inhaling. This has also been described as storing air in the gut, allowing a transfer of oxygen to the blood through the intestinal wall. This increases the efficiency of the breathing process. This is claimed to have a good influence on the general health of the practitioner: first heating and then cooling the body internally while promoting circulation and rejuvenation of the skin. The practitioner is also supposed to gain an acute awareness of his or her body functions, and if he or she continues the practice as an adjunct to meditation, he/she develops a familiarity with experiences that reverberate in the esoteric teachings of the main religions of the world.

From my experience of the meditative practice in *budo* (see *Path Notes*) I can say that these conjectures are all true. *Budo* as a religion has very few followers in these times, and even as a general term for the martial arts drawn from the warrior traditions that are considered ways or paths to martial enlightenment, it still cannot be described in any way as popular. There are seven million practitioners of some form of martial art in the United States. Nearly five million are involved in sport or tournament arts. That is a big market. Out of these about twelve thousand practice traditional *ninpo*. Of those twelve thousand about six hundred passed the *godan* test and five hundred become *shidoshi*. Of those five hundred *shidoshi* twenty manifest some of the characteristics of an enlightened *budo*man.

Usually, at least in Japanese *ryu*, the successor is the only one taught *chi kung* meditation and breath techniques for subtle influence. He passes the secrets on to his successor when he becomes aware of impending immortality. Hatsumi-soke occasionally discusses energy, life force, and their importance to *budo* in his *tai kai* videos. His video on the *naganata*, particularly the heavy *bisento* (big heavy sword for clobbering horses) segment, contains some vital remarks concerning breath skill, eating energy, and youthfulness, as well as remarks from his teacher Takamatsu-sensei. Muramatsu-sensei has been quite open with me. Some of the other Japanese *shihan* have asked their students to read my books and have exchanged knowing looks and tickles when we have trained together at seminars and *taikai* around the world. Those who study *bujinkan* and haven't made the journey to Japan for advanced training, particularly during these auspicious years, are missing an opportunity to experience true *budo*.

However, *bujinkan* politics and the Japanese aside, the internal or esoteric practice of breath and energy techniques that are associated with *budo* do exist in other forms such as Taoist *chi kung*, or, outside of China, Tibetan yoga, where the practice is called *Dumo*, or "heat yoga." In India, the practice is called *pranayama*, particularly *kumbakha*. The Western esoteric traditions in Greek and Russian Orthodox monasticism have a considerable body of knowledge concerning meditative breath practice under the heading of *pneuma*. Interestingly enough the gnostics (essenes, the cult Jesus and John the Baptist belonged to in Nazareth) considered a man or woman who had attained the control of *pneuma* (the fiery spirit that controlled the universe, breath, life, and energy as a psychic force stored in the brain and moved through the arteries) as *pneumatikos* or *perfecti*. The Greek word *prosevkomei* (prayer) means to be in a mindful state of awareness, not petitioning or verbalization of any sort. *Theoria* is paying attention without expectations, not contemplation.

By the eleventh century meditation had disappeared from the mainline teachings of the Roman Catholic church. The rituals and symbolism preserved by the Masonic lodges indicate that esoteric knowledge brought back from the Middle East during the Crusades was not entirely forgotten, but considering the fate of the Knights Templar, it was not discussed openly, which resulted in a loss of esoteric meanings, though the exoteric rituals and trappings remain for the enjoyment of the ritualists.

The non-Chinese Western and Japanese esoteric discussions and descriptions tend to be vague and allow for wild interpretation, as they seldom go beyond the naming of the technique. This guarantees that if you want the talent or knowledge you have to join the club. The Taoist library, on the sinister hand, is quite extensive and detailed. Thousands of books and exercises are drawn from the personal experience of the practitioners. The books deal with diet. They explain how the breath can be trained, refined, and even stopped for long periods of time. Also explained are breath techniques for curing diseases and ways of influencing internal organs, specific glands, or the entire endocrine system for beneficial effects. There are essays on postures to be assumed when sitting, standing, reclining, and even sleeping. The Taoists being essentially a hedonistic meritocracy (with both male and female lineages included), there are manuals of esoteric sexual practices that could be used to strengthen various organs while having a really good time.

The Chinese medical techniques for balancing and energizing the body's energy systems are usually easier to learn and less shrouded in secrecy than the techniques of the martial arts, since they are designed to be used by the sickly as opposed to the athletic. They also work better, and the descriptions are usually written by someone who understands the process and its effects, rather than someone who has been hit in the head many, many times and is trying to remember what his teacher showed him when he wasn't paying attention to the "right stuff." Fortunately there are people like Grandmasters Tom Muncy and Rick Moneymaker of *torite jutsu*, who have taken the time to apply a little scientific method to studying traditional Chinese medicine, the theoretical application of energy concepts to *tuite*, and have made their work available to the general martial art public. They teach a rudimentary form of *chi kung* and have worked out a system of pressure-point attacks based on acupuncture and the five-element theory that brings a lot of players to the game.

Intent

The development of physical techniques for training of intent or the spirit as a function of the breath can range from soldiers calling cadence as they run, to opera singers amplifying emotion through song, or esoterically projecting a feeling to another entity. At its most basic, fighting with the breath consists of screaming or exhaling as you strike and inhaling as you avoid. This gives you more strength and may frighten your opponent. It's pretty crude, and about all that is taught in most *dojo*. Fighting applications of the unrefined breath is a short topic of little interest when the real game for the martial artist is learning to refine the breath in order to obtain higher energy. The goal is twofold: controlling the breath leads to better health and greater endurance on the physical side, and if one pays attention to paying attention, the doorways of perception may also open a crack, allowing the light of a more cosmic vision to enter the warrior's realm. Esoteric breathing techniques enhance the experience of meditation and speed the practitioner's development of subtle energy and influence. They are not meant for use only in the *dojo* but for practice in the doing of one's life. To quote the venerable Miyamoto Musashi, "One must make the warrior walk his everyday walk." Musashi was referring more to attitude than a style of traipsing about. Hatsumi-soke is less opaque when he posits, "You must take the learnings of the *dojo* out into your life to test their value."

The gifts of true *giri* (duty to a real teacher) remain without price. You cannot learn to swim by practicing in the air, and falling in and surviving rarely (if ever) results in grace. Refining the breath into higher energy can be accomplished without encountering a guru or becoming a *deshi*, but it is definitely more difficult, particularly if your chosen spiritual path is *budo*. One must remember that most practitioners of martial arts (even *ninja*) are the equivalent of violence-fixated physical education instructors without degrees in how to teach. Subtlety is not their forte. Even icons of the *dojo* who have been competitors and teachers as long as I can remember completely miss the importance of meditation, mysticism, and proper deep belly breathing. I had one ancient and high-level *tae kwan do* practitioner ask me about some meditation techniques and then tell me the urban myth about students of meditation found dead sitting in *seiza* as an excuse for not deepening his experience. (No guts, no glory! Pun intended.)

The idea that one should meditate on one's death is a common religious and Buddhist concept. In some forms of *budo* one is remonstrated to act as if dead. This means to have no desire, particularly to live and fear, so that there is no hesitation in the response to the reality of the moment. This is the state of *mushin* (going with the flow) and there are better ways of achieving this state, also known as "divine emptiness" to the religious (*Fill me, O Lord. I am an empty vessel with no thought but your service*) than contemplating death and its effects. There is also *haragei* (spirit guts), the highest form of *kata* meditation in *karate. Haragei* is derived from the process of emptying the mind while following the breath, using the deep belly breathing techniques of *chi kung* while assuming various *kamae* (fighting stances) to move energy around the body.

The worn clichés and metaphors used in the martial arts recommend *jutsu* (skills) to approach the mountain, that to climb to the summit requires a *do* (way), but to reach the clouds above the summit one must invoke *ho* or *po* (water or spirit going forth or living). *Ho* in Sanskrit means realized, and in Chinese has the meaning of together, similar to the American "all together." *Ho* is the Chinese equivalent of the Japanese *po* (natural law) and can also mean weapon as well as truth and ocean *chi*. In the colloquial these are forms of the concept of androgyny or melding *in/yin* and *yo/yang* to achieve balance. *Bumon* (martial arts) and *shimon* (religious arts) combine in the training of the *bushi* (knight) or *shinobi* (enlightened warrior). *Ninpo*, when practiced as *budo*, was once considered the highest form of martial consciousness development that parallels religion. However, like Wiccans to Christians, the viewpoint of the dominant martial orders/*ryu* have demonized the ancient *ninpo* practices. The precepts of modern *budo taijutsu* are to develop the sensitivities of the human being to the point of being able to sense and respond to the universal energies of the life force. *Chi* is the life force and is with you always even in death.

Of course, learning to sense these movements of subtle energy takes a great deal of attention and sensitive concentration. Finding the proper wave can be an intense exercise in willpower. Don Juan, Carlos Castenada's mentor, used a complex but natural pharmacopoeia to jump-start him on the path of knowledge, and then gave young Castanada tasks such as sewing a lizard's eyes shut. Now that takes concentration, and I'll bet the lizard wasn't enthused. *Tensegrity* is very similar to *chi kung* in that some of its forms resemble *kata*. Impeccability was one of Don Juan's more favored concepts concerning the Yaqui path.

I think that affirmations enhance one's self-image and can be used to speed personal growth as well as to assimilate intentions into a worldview through meditation and self-hypnosis. Affirmations can be used to prepare the body for the onslaught of higher energy that accompanies kundalini arousal. The combination of physical activity appropriate to altered states of consciousness can enhance initiations into memorable rituals. In *hoshin* we memorialize the opening of chakra by using the principles of the *godai* imbedded in rituals that result in arousal.

You haven't really done the earth thing until you have emerged floundering out of an underground stream to experience the earth

24

meditations deep in the clay-slick stalactites and stalagmites of the Illinois Caverns with Frank Hagen's *hoshin* group in Springfield, Illinois. Greg Cooper's *bujinkan dojo* does the water element service by adventuring in the Atlantic on beautiful Cocoa Beach, Florida. Doing a floating meditation out past the surf brings home with power and clarity where we are on the food chain and how we stand with Mother Nature. There are many lessons beyond sword and fighting skills to be learned in the waves.

Geoff Smith's Sydney *dojo* fire-walk on the Johnson Ranch back in the gum forests of Australia where the bonfire loomed higher than my head was scarier than most. Stalking through the pristine park-like Hillsdale College Arboretum in Michigan while being hunted by the long-term *hoshin* practitioners and teachers Todd Smith and Tom Van Auken evokes the wind element as well as some fun paranoia. Robin Martin's *shinjinkan* (school for the human spirit) *dojo* in Lake Charles combines belt testing and sweat lodges for the healers more interested in *hoshintao chi kung* techniques. General training with Robin and teacher certification in both systems can be had at Lake Charles or any of the *hoshin dojo*. Robin and I work very closely and he probably knows my system better than I do. In fact, he has a better working knowledge of the martial arts biz than I, so we are getting ready to market the *hoshin* system on an international basis. Check out www.hoshin.com.

Kevin Millis-shihan and I used to take the *ninji* out cliff-hanging with an invitation to participate in "Dr. Morris's Bloody crucible of death." There were few takers on those ego-killing adventures back in the eighties, but we are all still friends. There is an esoteric school in *ninpo* named White Tiger Swallows Green Dragon, which translates from the esoteric symbolism as "after you have opened your powerful maleness (dragon) to the healing heart (green chakra), you will have to study to engulf this great power with white energy (head/lotus chakra) from the female side (tiger).

A story common to many martial arts is that a challenger enters the *dojo* and calls out to the master. An older, enthusiastic white belt who really isn't much of a fighter is so honked off by this rude behavior that he gets in the challenger's face and backs him down by appearing so willingly ferocious. The challenger apologizes and hurriedly departs; everyone in the *dojo* has a good laugh. Intent, not skill, wins the day.

Budo as a path for personal growth forces us to develop courage and endurance as the path has no destination beyond survival. The concept of survival of the fittest changes with the biological processes of living and dying as well as one's position in the social order and armament. Warriors who wish to be recognized as being better than a mere fighter (cannon fodder, no matter how skilled and seasoned, are still cannon fodder), must internalize compassion, humor, problem-solving abilities, objectivity, and leadership characteristics, while nurturing and improving the physical skills that attracted their interest in *budo* from the beginning. Nobody really gets into the martial arts for the discipline. We all start as white-belt fighters. After forty years some of us are still white-belt fighters no matter how many hashmarks we have on our black belts.

The esoteric Buddhist system of waking up the chakra through assuming attitudes and performing exercises *(godai)* alters the personality of the practitioner. The esoteric Taoist system of energy and orbits works even faster, particularly when combined with Zen sitting. From the viewpoint of a shamanistic participant and observer, I can attest that for those that actually do the work and assume the positions, the changes are beneficial. The difference in the Eastern goals of this sort of training from the Western benchmarks of alchemical magick are negligible. Even the external rituals that represent local color rather than biological necessity are often similar in meaning if not content.

There is an assumption in some schools of therapeutic psychology that the personality is not particularly malleable. This position is held by those who do not recognize the damaging effects of frustration and stress on the mechanisms of change. We develop a worldview through interaction and imitation. If our models are not particularly sophisticated, we develop challenges to overcome as part of our growth processes. If we truly wish to grow, we must change our worldview, not use our warped worldview as a tool to understand the other. To use a *godai* (five element or great principles) example: trying to develop a truly windy perspective from an earthy worldview only results in a pseudo-breeze, similar to a zephyr from the nether eye. This is the same mistake made in psychology when one observes the sociopath fitting smoothly into the daily interaction and conversation and believes that this slick presentation of self is the real persona rather than the created shadow. One of the reasons the Japanese do not teach the *kihon* (basic techniques for developing *chi*) from the perspectives of the *godai* is that it is too easy to lock into the comfort of remaining in one's dominant attitude rather than developing the egoless state most amenable to shifting up and down the internal scale as necessary to the external situations. The most common result of this blasphemous (Webster's secondary meaning) misinterpretation of psychological and transpersonal development are people half-baked by the internal fires who nonetheless believe the recipe resulted in a successful cook-out. Of course, half a loaf is better than no coffee break at all.

In *hoshintao chi kung* training and *hoshinjutsu,* the *godai* viewpoints are taught as biological-based assumptions from TCM (traditional Chinese medicine) to be modified or transformed through initiations and physical techniques. These reinforce strengths and then turn them into weaknesses to be challenged by the assumption of the next set of laws. The practitioner has to assume all the positions and transcend them to achieve freedom. Some of my *ninja* friends refer to what I do as Ninja Lite (less time—more fulfilling!), but *hoshin* is preparation, not completion and not *ninpo*. I send people into *ninpo* all the time and they learn very quickly that what I have given them is basic training, not the keys to the kingdom. Practitioners of *hoshin* can go into any *dojo* or *kwoon* anywhere in the world and train without fear of looking foolish, but if they desire mastery of any other system of self-protection they will find there are plenty of challenges to overcome or absorb.

Training of intention requires both imagination and attention. We pay attention to feelings to build our catalogue. We use our imagination to regulate intensity and projection. There is a visual component to projection that gives the advantage to the artist, architect, or engineer. We use our breath to build endurance, power, and accuracy. The use of weaponry adds a dimension of realism to training, particularly to avoidance skills, that results in razor-edge focus and control. The use of role-playing and theatrics can enhance one's ability to understand others as well as the self. It is said in holy scripture that the higher level is invisible to the lower level. Study on that.

CHAPTER THREE

The Shadow, Eros, and Thanatos

Du bliebst der Konig—auch in Unterhosen (You are the king—even in your underwear).
> —Ludwig Fulda, writer, *The Talisman,* 1893

Understanding human needs is half the job of meeting them.
> —Adlai Stevenson, unsuccessful presidential candidate, speech in 1952

It's good to be king!
> —Tom Petty, very successful rock musician, contemporary

"The Way of the Samurai Is Found in Death"

This famous phrase from the *Hagekure (Hidden Leaves)* commentaries of Yamamoto Tsunetomo as collected by the unemployed scribe Tashiro Tsuramato (the incredible recorded by the unhirable), on Yamamoto's unhappy life as a clerical samurai of the Nabeshima clan, has touched a resonating chord in the minds of many modern martial artists. As Yamamoto did not know his words were being collected by the idling scribe, he did not censor his thoughts but spoke from the heart with single-minded fervor. It is a shame that he was so rigid and dark of spirit that he longed for death. He was forbidden *seppuku* or *junji* (ritual suicide from grief over a master's death), the ultimate form of sucking up to the family by the Tokugawa *shogunate*. This extreme radical retired unhappily, shaving his ponytail to become a Buddhist priest where his vision of hell would be mildly acceptable. His relieved wife became a nun.

I have never heard quoted Yamamoto's opening to his second chapter, "sake, self-pride, and luxury are to be avoided by a samurai," or the empathetic "a person who becomes fatigued when unhappy is useless," at least not in *ninja* circles. My favorite quote from *Hidden Leaves* is, "It is good to carry some powdered rouge in one's sleeve. It may happen that when one is sobering up his complexion may be poor. At such a time it is good to take out and apply some powdered rouge." In fact, the Boss (Hatsumi-soke) is the only Japanese I have met who can actually discuss the *Hagekure* intelligently, and he doesn't like it much. The Boss is the titular head of six famous *samurai ryu* as well as the infamous three surviving *ninja ryu*, all subsumed to some extent in his presentation of *bujinkan budo taijutsu*.

Thanatos

Sigmund Freud, a great psychiatrist who made some wild errors in psychological theory, would have regarded Yamamoto as one possessed by the Greek god Thanatos. Freud would have been dead on the numbers for Yamamoto Tsunetomo.

Freud's *thanatos* stood for the generalized instinct for death, as expressed in such behaviors as denial, rejection, and the turning away from pleasure. The death wish is common to martial arts practitioners, manifesting itself through the failure to achieve and its close cousin perfectionism, which is based in the fear of failure. For the intelligent death-seeker every aspect of life must be in order to avoid the embarrassment of finding oneself left for dead alongside the road with stained underwear revealed. Servants who skillfully copy the robotic moves of their masters are not too different from martial technicians, or, as my very acerbic *buyu* (martial arts friend or colleague in arms), computer wizard, actor, and stuntman Lonie Hilton of Toronto refers to them, "born-again technicians." His statement berates many of the teachers of the *ryu* to widen their experience to ensure the preservation of the worth of the *ryu,* even if it means living in the halls of the competition or studying with teachers other than where they started. This is particularly true after *godan.*

When the warrior ego and superego regard Death's shadow, there is a feeling of loss of what should have been. "Why was I born in such a lifeless age? Where are the challenges to match my fettle? Who will sing my story round the campfire centuries from now? I long to hear the clash of swords!" may translate into the current incarnate milieu as "Why can't I get a job I really like?" or, "Hawcum I ain't got no respect?"

Often the death seeker has a feeling of being born in the wrong time or place and regularly reports experiences of déjà vu. Because the times are not right, the he or she is drawn to ritual and hierarchy as a stabilizing factor in a world that has no standards of excellence worthier than those espoused by the *hombu.* Only his or her particular martial art is worthy of study; the seeking student need seek no more, since everything is already here. This narrows perspective and leads to a limited eco-niche resulting in extinction as the world changes and the *ryu* does not.

Even the professionals of war regard their position as death-bringers wryly. As the marching song "Oh, you knuckleheads" fore-tells one's doom, so too do the running cadences of endless refrains, "Ain't no sense in lookin' back! Jody's got yo Cadillac. Ain't no use in feelin' blue. Jody's got yo girlfrien' too!" Airborne ranger Jody calls are similar to the cautionary tales of the coyote trickster in Native Amer-ican mythology. The warnings to the trainees seldom register above the subconscious as the modern equivalent to the *samurai* is molded and hardened into grade-A government-inspected cannon fodder.

In the film *The French Lieutenant's Woman,* one of the protago-nists swears another to secrecy on a copy of Darwin's *Origin of Species.* It had more meaning then; they were farther into white supremacy in those halcyon days of Victorian blood and thunder leading to the red-coated Charge of the Light Brigade. Eugenics as an attempt to fool Mother Nature. There are still those willing to die for glory, the old blood, the cold blood not totally thinned. They used to make bombs in Michigan, but now hide and burn crosses in Idaho.

Eros

Freud balanced the death lover with the life-seeking lover Eros, the Greek god of love. Eros for Freud represented the complex of life-preservative instincts, including, of course, sexual needs and drives. Freud believed that creativity was related to sexual frustration as opposed to a learned way of thinking about events and things. His frustration concept is one of his grayer areas of thinking; however, it may coincide with one's youthful exuberance and willingness to do almost anything to impress the object of one's affection. Approval may not be as strong a motivator as getting laid, but it comes close for the neurotic.

Loving what you do enough to continually seek improvement is far different motivation than perfecting what you do as if death were the payment for being wrong. The negative-thinking realist will perceive the latter pattern as being wiser and will continue to inten-sify his or her practice out of fear. The lover's practice may be just as intense, but the feeling of the practice is without frenzy or reactivity.

When I was doing a seminar in Trinidad with some American Grandmasters, one of the participants came up to me and said, "You are very different from these other great martial artists! You laugh when you do techniques, and you sang our national anthem. Are all *ninja* like you?" It was a fair question. I couldn't answer it. About a month later the huge guy that we all used in the class as *uke* (punching dummy and throw monkey) won the Caribbean's heavyweight kickboxing title. He said what gave him the edge was something I had shown him. I don't have a clue what that was.

The warrior as artist develops a different mind-set because an artist is concerned with the discipline of presenting his or her own interpretation of some form of presentation skill. The warrior-scholar studies the lives and statements of those who have survived under the various conditions that an interesting life will force on adventure seekers. The burgeoning warrior seeks a mentor, and through interaction with that person learns the basics as well as the advanced techniques the mentor is willing to part with. He or she may join a *dojo* and participate in traditional training. He or she may take part in seminars offered by skilled masters with international reputations to enhance skills.

This presupposes that the presenting master is teaching something worth learning. I have overheard my students vilify nationally known "experts" after paying outrageous fees for what they considered minimal technique and worse information at a seminar, and felt a twinge of shame knowing that the "experts" were ranked higher than I am. One can achieve high ranks through cross-ranking. Someone who got their rank that way really should not offer open seminars. In most martial arts, ranks after *godan* (fifth-level black belt) are considered administrative and political rather than technical in nature. I was told by George Anderson that all degrees after fifth were administrative, as far as the Japanese were concerned. George is the American *soke* of *Seibukan*, a famous Japanese *karate ryu*. American *ninja* are often ranked higher than their Asian counterparts, as *giri* (duty/respect/devotion) is not a well-understood concept in our culture. *Shidoshi* Mark O'Brien, who has lived and trained in Japan

33

throughout the twelve years I've known him, admits to *godan* and even acts insulted when asked what his "real" rank in the *booj* might be.

The inability to recognize the relative importance of one's inconsequential position in the timeline of the universe leads one to puff up the self-esteem. Facing the sword with regularity should reduce the compulsion to arrogance in inadequate individuals. There was a time in *ninjutsu* when *shidoshi* were required to return to the Grandmaster at regular intervals to take the sword test with a live sword. Those that failed died or were horribly scarred. It is suggested that this was a method for removing those whose egos could not allow them to submit, as well as a process for continually testing the purity of heart. (If I were Hatsumi-soke, I'd renew that ritual as part of *tai kai* [annual gathering], but I'm afraid the ranks would thin enormously. Maybe a *bokken* test every five years?) Hatsumi-soke has instituted a form of interesting peer review. If ten or more students lodge a formal complaint against a teacher, *bujinden* (*hombu* or the big dogs) will investigate. If the accusers prevail, the accused will be struck from the rolls.

I have noticed that every high-ranking *ninja* that has departed *bujinkan* or surreptitiously altered the style of training and teaching to suit their own needs, begins after a fairly short period of time to exhibit a marked decline in physical skill and flexibility. The perceptive regard this as a strange sort of "bad *ninja* go away" curse but the reality is the standards of comparison of the departed become polluted and egocentric when they haven't the Boss to challenge them. The obverse is also true. Some of the people I regarded as relatively hopeless years ago (with *taijutsu* even worse than mine and personalities to laugh at behind their backs) through their continual attendance of training sessions with the Boss have become far more interesting human beings; I can now introduce them to my friends and send them students. The teaching has also improved. A decade or so ago we were a dangerous lot, and often pushed the envelope for our students, giving them near-death experiences instead of adapting to their level.

The central tenet of innumerable religions is to stamp out the pretensions of the ego, but those craving a higher sense of meaning though unwilling to do the actual work will go to monstrous lengths to reinforce their ego. ("Follow me. I am the way, the truth, and the light," sounds suspiciously like "I'm the only one who knows how to teach this art successfully.") When you hear that kind of talk, take a quick look around for the collection agents. My students have been out in the world for some five or ten years now, mixing with our old enemies as well as fear, blight, and rejection. Some survive to report what they have learned in other martial arts.

Yin and Yang

How can the back be allergic to the front?
If the front attacks does the back repel?
If the back attacks can the front absorb?
Why does external pain increase when you follow the yang?
Why does internal pain increase when you interrupt the yin?
When the opponent shows emptiness, be cautious and loving.
When the opponent extends power, take it, eat it, and return it
    tenfold.

CHAPTER FOUR

The Gurus of Death Archetypes

*Im ewigen Kampfe ist die Menschheit gross gewor-
den—im ewigen Frieden geht sie zugrunde. (In eternal
struggle manliness grows strong—in eternal peace it
will perish.)*

> —Adolph Hitler, sorry soldier, bad writer,
> failed painter, skilled politician,
> and highly successful megalomaniac
> and mass murderer, *Mein Kampf,* 1924

*Debbe adunque uno principe non avere altro obietto
ne altro pensiero, ne prendere cosa alcuna per sua
arte, fuora della guerra e ordini e disciplina di essa;
perche quella e sola arte chi se espetta a chi comanda.
(Therefore a prince should have no other aim or
thought, nor any hobby or study, but the study of the
organization and discipline of war. War is the only art
necessary to one who commands.)*

> —Niccolo Machiavelli, failed rhetorician,
> *Il Principe,* 1532

We make war that we may live in peace.

> —Aristotle, successful rhetorician,
> *Nichomachean Ethics,* circa 325 B.C.E.

Guru or Sensei

Archetypes can be considered a mystical and mythic representation of the human demiurge similar to *drala* or *kami* and in the martial arts are often reduced to the stereotypical. The Thanatos syndrome has a greater attraction for the negative-thinking warrior. There is a strong need to die gloriously, to be the "top or fastest gun," or to know the deadly secrets, and those of us who watch the immortals of *The Highlander* know there can only be one! In many otherwise sane and normal people, Thanatos occupies a need for renown and danger. Most of our lives are humdrum enough that we buy into these minor inanities out of the need for wish fulfillment. The typologies I see most often are explained below so that martial arts consumers can increase their awareness of what they are buying. One of the reasons I can explain these stereotypes is I have lived them at various times in my development as a martial artist. I am not particularly proud of this knowledge, but over the years I have learned to accept and live with my scars, and perhaps somewhat sheepishly take a little perverse pride and nurture a dark laughter from them.

In the martial arts there are ways of approaching the reality of teaching that appeal to certain strengths and weaknesses in the students/observers/audience. These are like the tired sales pitches of the carny barker, and some are clear indicators to the clued-in that we/you are dealing with a case of what the Boss calls "martial arts madness." As I said in the introduction, I draw my examples from the martial arts in which I have studied. Names are usually withheld to protect the guilty, but I'm sure some of my readers will get a gasp and chuckle at some of the clinical discussion in this and the next chapter.

The Death-Seeking-Warrior Syndrome

There is probably no need to describe the reality of the thirsting motivation that drives martial artists to join the military so that they can practice their art. The problem is the military martial art of America is the pistol, plane, and mechanical monster. We are nothing if not deadly but the skills of hand-to-hand are a very low priority in this age of modern mayhem topped by a nuclear cloud. Having an ex-Marine, SEAL, Green Beret, Ranger, Delta, Recondo, SAS, or other elite commando-type as an instructor is no guarantee of low-tech martial art skill—or teaching ability—in this age of push-button and automatic weaponry. I've reviewed most elite military training over the years and bar-brawled with more than a few in my youth, and with the exception of the World War II Quick Kill course (Defendu) developed by the Brits out of Hong Kong, I am not impressed.

Practically all martial artists go through a stage of "killer-elite-wanna-be" before realizing that is a very small and overrated arena that is to be avoided like death itself. Why put to risk all the potential of one's life for the short rewards of war? There is both always and never a good day to die. If all you have left is your hand-to-hand skills, somebody up the food chain made a major mistake concerning your mission and supplies. It is like receiving a medal for calling in rocket and artillery fire on your own position when it is being overrun by the enemy (the American equivalent of ritual suicide in the infantry). Think about it.

I've had many ex-elite commando types study with me over the years and I have talked with many of my *ninpo* and *kung fu* instructors who have attracted ex-military elite, and we all agree that what is taught in the civilian *dojo* of a senior instructor far exceeds the quick and dirty methods prized by the military, particularly when we are discussing unarmed or very low-tech combat. Doing one's hitch might provide an opportunity to test one's courage or at par one's ability to endure boredom. It may not be wise, but neither is patriotism. Sam Colt would have loved an F-17 and absolutely marveled at an aircraft carrier.

The Jean-Claude-Killing-Machine Syndrome

Every decade has a martial-artist-as-entertainer superstar that inspires others to imitation. Imitation of an actor is not the sincerest form of flattery, it is stupid. This is why a favorite U.S. Marine motto is "John Wayne Is Dead." And when a DI yells, "Who do think you are, John Wayne?" (or James Bond in the intelligence biz) it is not a compliment. For real martial artists, claiming a relationship to a movie star is very iffy business, unless said star is trying to learn some real techniques from the instructor. I've been in *dojo* that had movie posters on the wall, yet there was no obvious relationship with the actor as some sort of associative salesmanship. That sort of thing makes me want to puke. I even know a guy who changed his name to Bruce. It was a long reach.

Jackie Chan, trained from childhood in Chinese opera, is one of the best martial artists to ever make a movie, and for the longest time no one took him seriously because he had a sense of humor. Even Bruce Lee had the film speeded up as he grew older (he wasn't that old), and let us not forget why stuntmen are paid big bucks to make the star look heroic. People like stories and someone is always creating urban mythology such as Bruce Lee being killed by Chinese *ninja,* or Jean Claude Van Damme being a real martial artist/fighter as opposed to an actor/dancer/uncertified massage giver. Judo practitioner Gene LaBell has contributed stuntmen to the movie industry for thirty years and is respected by everyone as a world-class *judoka.* Stuntmen, not the actors, are often the real martial artists in a movie. Chuck Norris presents the arts positively. Jeff Speakman, Dolf Lundgren, and Stephen Seagal have paid their martial art dues on a more limited level. I have yet to see *ninpo* presented with anything resembling reality on television or the movies in the United States.

The Dangerous-Human Syndrome

This is similar to the above, but the association is not with stardom and whatever that may entail in the mind of the martial artist wanna-be but with the lethality of one's skills. I don't know how many young mercenary-hitmen-assassin part-timers I've broken bread with over the years, particularly between wars, who have pumped me for employment opportunities. "When I'm not washing cars, I'm a hitman for the Tong, Triad, yaks, mob, whatever, or whomever can pay my freight." Thanatos extends a bony finger and beckons the whispering worshipper to enter the temple of doom and delusion.

If I were really in that line of work I certainly wouldn't talk about it to a relative stranger, particularly one who occasionally trains police departments. Often these delusionaries discuss their training with the CIA or DEA as being undercover or secret and thus untraceable, i.e., "I used an assumed name when I worked for Special Operations." Gimme a break, I'm an old man! When I was a young man, it was survivors of Phoenix and mildly deranged Vietnam vets that were all the rage, so I even talked some of that trash myself. "I did it because I was a Marine/Korean/Vietnam vet/friend of OJ!" was almost as good an excuse as "It just came out of me," or, "The devil made me do it."

When I was in grad school some of my colleagues felt I suffered from what was then called combat fatigue by the polite, and shell shock by the rude. It is very odd to me now that at that age I had this need to be thought of by others as a suffering and dangerous individual. I was fortunate in having friends who cared more about me than I did myself. It seemed fun at the time, part of the twelve-step program for recovering from military-induced machismo. The Vietnam war was winding down. The peace movement was becoming the antidraft movement. The sexual revolution was in full bloom. I owe a lot to my college girlfriends, as they were friends indeed and treated me far better than I deserved. Anyone who thinks being thought of as dangerous is an advantage in this age of concealed weaponry doesn't really understand the advantage of surprise and the usefulness of discretion.

The Ultimate-Martial-Art Syndrome

Practically everybody who takes or teaches a martial art would prefer not to think that their skills are easily destroyed by a shrouded hammer pocket pistol, usually referred to as a "chief's special." Nevertheless it is true. A lawyer once asked me what I thought the most dangerous martial arts were. I replied, *"budo taijutsu,* some schools of *gong fu,* but the ultimate is a person with a hidden Glock .40." He was smart enough to agree. If you have to mix your art with something else to make it work, it ain't the One. If you have to practice for many years to achieve combat-appropriate skills, it ain't either. If it relies on strength, speed, or athleticism, it is a sport. If it doesn't include weaponry and at least show you how to use firearms there is a fatal flaw in how the founder perceived the Darwinian influence on technology and social change. The ancient Chinese included things in their training of the warrior that went boom and sprayed jagged edges, and through most of Japanese history both the *ninja* and occasionally the *samurai* used and developed firearms or distance weapons. The ancient samurai loathed modern weaponry and eventually fell to it. Theirs was also the only culture to adopt firearms and then reject them. The insane rejection was primarily because a peasant could learn to use one with ease, and they were so graceless to handle and use!

Most physical martial systems have been so influenced by attempts to popularize them by narrowing the techniques to watered-down representations that they require a skilled and helpful *uke* to appear awesome and are easily blown away by someone who has a real feel for combat. I remarked in my first book that the stick fighting of *kali* didn't impress me. Since then I've run into some higher-level practitioners who use knives instead of sticks, which makes the art much more exciting. The sticks were for practice and beginners. There is a big difference between playing with Grandmaster Ernesto Presas Sr. and Joe Blow from Boise, Idaho. Escrima is not to be sneered at, at least by me.

The ultimate in martial arts has little to do with physical techniques. *Heiho* (strategy) is the martial art that is generally recognized as closest to the top of the mountain regardless of the lineage, and *tai chi* is the most universally accepted as ultimate due to its relationship to *chi* and longevity. *Chi kung* is the hidden core of *tai chi* that is missed by so many teachers of that marvelous health-enhancing combat system.

Keeper-of-the-Master's-Secrets Syndrome

Exaggeration of one's skills or the skills of one's teacher (or the closeness of one's relationship to the teacher) are common rhetorical devices to attract more students to a particular martial school. These tired ploys are also well rehearsed by *chi kung* wanna-bes and religious practitioners who guarantee a personal relationship with the founder no matter how long dead and/or distantly removed. The crap I have heard concerning "my teacher" is probably only topped by what "I have been shown" and will gladly impart after you have kissed my arse for ten or twenty years. Watch real close for a while before you buy into that one. Last week a fat *nidan* from *tae kwan do* introduced himself to me as a fellow martial artist, told me of his sparring with Jean-Claude when he was in Texas years ago (this kid is twenty-two or twenty-three), and how his Vietnamese (?) master of TKD at age eighty-one could knock him across the room with an energy strike. Of course the old boy had returned to his maker last year. (He had probably died of shame.)

It is amusing to many of us in the *bujinkan* to see pictures of first Takamatsu, then Hatsumi, and then some American as if he or she were the third coming or linear successor. Often when the lineages are listed in a Western or American *bujinkan* newsletter there will be the name of a poseur inserted like a daisy among the devil's paintbrushes.

Everyone at or above the rank of *godan* is Hatsumi's personal student, whether they (or outsiders) realize it or not. In this way the pictorial triumvirate can resemble the truth, but too many of the naive take this as a representation of succession. In the early nineties Hatsumi-soke listed me in Japan as his successor in the United States (whatever that might have meant to him) according to Richard Kimhanshi, who went out of his way to meet me because of this. Kimsensei said, "We have heard of Stephen Hayes, Bud Malmstrom, and Ralph Severe, but no one knows who you are." I was dumbfounded. It suddenly became clear why Daron Navon was always so deferential around me when I was studying with him. He is fluent in Japanese (I thought he was exceedingly polite, even for a good man). It would have been extremely detrimental to the *ryu* if something had happened to the Boss and I had to take that role. The only reason for the appointment was that I could teach the Japanese inheritor how to develop his *ki (chi)* and connect him to the *bujin* (*bujinkan's* guiding spirits). I'm quite certain that the Boss no longer worries about that particular problem, but you can tell from the risk he was willing to take that knowing how to teach and pass on *chi* was important to him. A lot can happen in seven years, and given that the Japanese could easily soil the escutcheons of the perfidious of Albion when it comes to setting up smoke screens and shifting loyalties under the guise of misunderstanding, there is no sane reason to conjecture if Dr. Morris is still considered for that role (I'm not).

Often when a senior practitioner finally reaches the masters rank, they forget the generous teachings of those who went before and begin to parse out their teachings and ranks as if Scrooge had been their patron. This is usually an indication that they have plateaued in knowledge and are keeping their students in a holding pattern to squeeze out a few more shekels. This behavior, sometimes imitative of how they were mistreated, just creates bitterness and is bad for the *ryu* or *kwoon*. Money and politics have choked off many a budding branch.

People often pretend that the higher rank indicates exclusivity of promotional rights. In the *booj*, after fifth only the Boss promotes, before fifth any *shidoshi* (licensed teacher who has passed the sword test) can promote a practitioner for any reason, so long as half the fee goes back to Noda. Some like to pretend that the Boss maintains a strict hierarchy in rank. "You can only be promoted by me, and no one can outrank me as I was first in this country," but I have seen no evidence of this in Australia, Europe, Japan, or the United States. I very seldom promote anyone in *bujinkan,* but when I have made a request it was always granted.

Hatsumi-soke's laissez-faire management style is more Darwinian than supportive. Hatsumi-san is a liberal democrat in the Jeffersonian sense of no racism, the rewarding of merit, and equal opportunity. This is quite different from the emphasis on rules, protocol and rigid hierarchical structure of some samurai/militaristic Japanese and Korean schools, but then the physical basis as well as underlying *bujinden* philosophy for *bujinkan budo taijutsu* comes out of the three *ninja ryu*, not the six *samurai ryu*. (If Tannemura actually were the head of the *bujinden,* it would not be an organization that I could live with, at least with a straight face. Now that he claims grandmastery over nine schools of *samurai jujutsu,* his stiff body movement, unfortunate *uke* aside, looks more appropriate to his supposed calling. The rumor that he was asked to leave the Tokyo police over issues concerning sadism seem borne out by the anger in what he chooses to show. Of course, given what I get accused of, who cares. People seem to get the teacher they deserve; like attracts like.

Some of the *shidoshi* act as if the Boss had signed their adoption papers in Japan, but they are just another fish in the stream when they enter *noda*. It is difficult for a Grandmaster to avoid sycophants, particularly in a culture that rewards rather than decries sucking up to the Boss. I have heard the Boss jokingly describe some masters' best skills as suckish. Such people go to a lot of trouble to have pictures of themselves hanging with the big guys. Always check out the picture for the Mona Lisa look. Is he really smiling? The Boss believes that pictures reveal the soul. Sometimes he is laughing at, rather than with. You must examine the eyes. What is he doing with his hands? Is he holding the person or showing a fist? He is a wonder.

Here's a story about Jack Nicklaus. A friend of mine was playing in a Pro-Am tournament. He partnered up with the golden one. For weeks afterward it was all we heard about. Finally I asked him how Mr. Nicklaus felt about playing with him. He flushed and then said, "He says it puts his game off for about a week to play at the amateur level." Jack didn't get brought up again.

It is helpful for the neophyte to remember that part of his training is to become perceptive enough to identify those teachers who can actually guide him or her in the way. There are few who understand spiritual development, regardless of their *taijutsu* skills. One of the funnier disclaimers I hear in *bujinkan* is that *taijutsu* represents spiritual skill. This is not heresy but fallacy. The vehicle is

45

different from the horse that pulls it. I have found that playing *tai-jutsu* with someone who really knows what they are doing jacks up my *jujutsu* skills as well as improves my *taijutsu,* since I spend a lot of time teaching in seminars and grooming up the white belts.

As I can't get to Japan as much as I would like, I try to find a skilled teacher among the younger guys just coming back from spending a couple of years there, like Greg Cooper or one of the older *shidoshi* such as Greg Kowalski, who has the skills to emulate the Boss. Dick Severance (older than dirt) and Richard Cearly (young and naive) are two *shidoshi* that can have you scratching your head in amazement. Dave Bolin in Houston is one of my favorite teachers because he has a real life. One of the reasons I don't teach traditional *taijutsu* is that there are far better teachers of that skill than I, and I prefer to learn from them (that does not mean that I am without advanced skills). Mark O'Brien's *taijutsu* is as good as it gets, though he is about esoteric as a duck. The Boss has asked me to open a *dojo* and I will, but I will hire out the teaching of the basics to some real *ninja.*

One of the major differences between beginning and advanced skills is that the long striding and deep body movements with a straight back disappear into the subtle twist of the hip and fluidity of the spine that accomplishes the same but cannot be identified as *taijutsu* except by the most sophisticated observer. The skills of the older practitioner are held tight to the body and are seldom seen outside of Japan or performed by anyone with under ten years of continual experience in the game, unless they have paid close attention to Dick Severance, Ed Martin, Shiraishi, or the Boss. The *omote* is for the youth, and the *ura* comes into play with experience. This seems to be true of other martial arts as well.

Tournaments of Sacrifice and Salvation

When you walk into a *dojo* and see huge trophies and a wall of smaller ones, take into consideration that trophies don't cost much, and hundreds are given away to first- through third-place winners at any large tourney. It doesn't take too long to acquire a bunch, particularly if you let your students display theirs in your *dojo*. It also helps if you are the guy who buys them in the first place.

Tournament fighting and one-point sparring are very different from a real fight. The skills for winning tournaments won't get you home to Momma on the street. Too often *dojang* and *dojo* only hold tournaments for their own students. This is poor practice and narrows the experience of the practitioner.

I have commented in my first two books on how tournaments are basically advertisements for schools and do little to develop the character of students. I have even had young tournament fighters ask me if I can tell from their auras when they are faking getting hit to win points through taking a foul. I nod knowingly, of course. Teachers who make a big deal out of tournaments are usually making a nice profit out of them. It is very difficult to keep a *dojo* alive in the United States if you do not hold some form of competitive tourneys, because "Amerikans" like to win.

The other guys who flip me out are the ones who think doing the same technique ten thousand times has something to do with discipline. *Henka* (variations) is the name of the survival and winning game, not *kata* (forms). Building up huge calluses on *makawari* boards is a waste of time when you can buy sap gloves. There is value in doing *kata* to enhance one's flexibility or open one's meridian lines, but if you do it for fighting, anyone who knows your *kata* knows your moves. We tend to do what we learned first, or what we are rewarded for. This goes for only studying with one teacher, too.

Martial Master as Sex Stud

As the homely Dr. Kissinger once remarked concerning his dalliance with the ladies of Washington and New York, "Power is the best aphrodisiac." Women can usually feel and work *chi* more efficiently than men. They are attracted subconsciously to the energy as a subtle biological indicator of the ability to produce superior offspring, even when there is no social reason for the attraction or conscious awareness of the energy. Both men and women develop a realistic confidence that increases attractiveness as their skills in combat are enhanced. The same is true of any athlete, because being in shape is an aid to sexual performance and health is associated with attractiveness. Now that I am twice the age of most of my martial colleagues, I am grateful that occasionally women find it interesting to help me keep my balance.

I noticed after an acupuncture session that morning erections had returned, and mentioned it to my acupuncturist Cheng De Wu. He chuckled and said, "We are young too." I watch carefully where he puts the needles now. *Gong shing-yi* includes a group of exercises called "happy woman techniques" that are performed by men for that result. Taoist *chi kung* happily includes exercises for seminal retention as well as organ rejuvenation through movement of energy. Tantra includes many fun things for a couple to practice. To my awareness *ninpo* has no specific practices that are taught, but the average *ninja* is above average in intelligence and usually researches things that are obviously useful and exciting.

When the *chi* begins to manifest strongly, it must be remembered that *jing* (sexual energy) is a major component! That is why many black belts go through a studmuffin phase, which often leads to disasters such as raping students, seducing the wives in their *dojo,* or blowing it all in the tittie bars. It must be remembered that many of these young men have devoted their lives to their concept of *budo* and don't have much skill in negotiation. Lust is mistaken for love, and seduction is equated with romance. I won't make a list, but most of us can name a few masters who stepped on their cranks. If your teacher includes sexual overtures as part of his or her package of instruction, he or she is supposed to be big enough to handle rejection, too. There are ways to increase the understanding of tantra through martial applications, but the real teachers are few and far between.

The Dangers of Following

In Western religious tradition the master too often leads followers into martyrdom. In the martial arts, martyrdom is usually on a small scale (I got stabbed in the parking lot), but the followers of Heaven's Gate, Bo and Peep, Charles Manson, Jim Jones, and David Koresh are easy to identify from a distance and hindsight. Manson, Jones, and Koresh were obsessed by power and the need to exert it. They enjoyed the despotic role, including sexual abuse, sadism, and complete conviction in their delusions. Like real martial artists, they were unequivocally dangerous. Bo and Peep appeared saintly in an out-of-this-world manner.

I don't see a great deal of difference in how some religious true believers act and how some martial-art practitioners act. As a psychologist and phenomenologist, and probably the only secular shaman you are likely to discover in the arena of psychology and *budo*, I tend to keep a "some of their pronouncements are not to be cast in stone" box for luminaries such as Gurdjieff, Krishnamurti, Steiner, Jung, Freud, Rajneesh, Einstein, Brunton, Plato, Aristotle, heads of martial art families, any organized religion that requires tithe or clergy, and most governments, including our own. I have been described by some of my Native American friends as having a "coyote" mentality. (They come for treatment anyhow, as an open mind is hard to find.) Like W.C. Fields I am free of prejudice and willing to attack all that I loathe on an equal-opportunity basis. If it is not your pet peeve's turn today, it may be tomorrow. I become crankier as Alzheimer approaches.

I have studied under a lot of people but have never found anyone I was willing to declare an exclusive and binding relationship to as a *deshi* (disciple). I usually tried to give as good as I got *(giri)*. When people check me out, the former teacher's kinder response might be, "Oh, yeah, Morris . . . yes, he used to study under me. Haven't seen him for a long time." I've never been a very good follower and often get ahead of both the times and myself. The "used to" needn't indicate an unhappy parting, it just means I got what I wanted and continued my quest for collegiality. My leadership traits are similar. When you follow my path you are pretty much on your own.

As an observer of people it isn't always easy to delineate where idiosyncratic belief systems turn from crank ideas to delusional ones. There are irrational belief systems that are shared and have survived in societies for thousands of years. Galileo challenged the idea of the Earth being the center of the universe and was attacked. It is unreasonable to exclude the idea of the masses sharing in a delusion. Just because there are many adherents doesn't mean the belief isn't delusional. When I was a kid it was generally believed that the four-minute mile was impossible for human beings. Now even high-school runners have broken that barrier. There is no magic.

Gymnastic God of Weapons Syndrome

Lao Tzu said the love and embellishment of weapons sanctifies disaster. Learning to use many of the ancient weapons can teach you skills and perceptions that you would never acquire any other way. However, the showy leaping-and-twirling skills of the tournament buff will get you shot down like a dog anywhere the concealed weapon laws are radical. Indiana Jones had the right of it, the first time.

Faithfulness to Teachers

In *budo* the title *sensei* (teacher) also translates as "one who has gone before," meaning your teacher has already traversed the path you wish to tread and is thus a reliable guide. "Reliable" implies a guarantee that if you think his or her guidance is less than masterful, it's quite all right to seek guidance elsewhere. If it appears your teacher has little of the knowledge of spiritual matters common to your circle of acquaintances, even if he or she has a masterful command of physical techniques, *dojo*, has great costumes, and would like you stay and train indefinitely for your pleasure and their training fee, quest is an acceptable form of departure for a *deshi* who promises to someday return with the loot he has ripped off of other forms of teaching. Returning is not mandatory.

50

Quest is the search for truth through experience and can be a test of one's skills of perception, as well as of one's force of arms. The goal of the quest is chivalrous enterprise and adventure, usually requiring a long journey. The search for a true martial-arts master of *budo* is supposed to be like a quest, and Hatsumi has created a marvelous maze for the civil and unwary that is international in nature and knows no boundaries. (There is a saying that you must never completely trust a martial arts "master," and that homily particularly applies to some who claim to be associated with, attended, and graduated *bujinkan* training.) It can be a *budoka's* (serious practitioner's) worst nightmare to discover that there are other teachers who make their *sensei* appear ego-driven and ignorant, if not suffering from martial art madness. When your teacher informs you that all you need to know is within the *dojo* walls or here in the States, take it with salts. When your teacher warns you not to study with others, claiming that it will ruin your form, particularly when you study something with depth and variation like *karate* or *jujutsu,* that is a red flag.

You must remember why you chose this path. Endurance means that you are expected to continue playing until you die or succeed in achieving enlightenment. (You are allowed to retire when training a successor, because of bitterness at your own failure, or in joy because you really don't feel any need to do this boring, archaic, dangerous tradition anymore.) Any other reason might be considered betrayal to some little or large extent, for like the *bodhi* (Sanskrit for multiples of Buddha), you are supposed to fulfill the *budo* law of *giri* by teaching others how you managed to pull it off so they can see if what worked for you will work for them. You are supposed to thank your teacher, if you had one. The quest for a personal truth is important (I must know that this is true).

If you are going to have someone tell you how to live, be certain they know more about living than you do. Most martial artists don't have what I would call a life. When entering the master/student religion—oops—relationship—one should look carefully at who is dependent on whom.

CHAPTER FIVE

Budo Transcendence: Warriors of Light

Un general victorieux n'a point fait de fautes aux yeux du public, de meme que le general battu a toujours tort, quelque sage conduit qu'il ait eue. (A victorious general has no faults in the eyes of the public, while a defeated general is always wrong no matter how wise his conduct may have been.)
>—Voltaire, wit, writer, musician, and playwright,
>*Le Siecle de Louis XIV,* 1751

Sich wehrlos machen, wahrend man der Wehrhafeste war, aus einer Hohe der Empfindung heraus, —das ist Mittel zum wirklichen Frieden welcher immer auf einem Frieden der Gessinung ruhen muss. (To give up one's arms, when one is the best armed, for a higher cause—that is the means to a real peace, which must first rest on peace of mind.)
>—Friedrich Nietzche, philosopher,
>*The Wanderer and His Shadow,* 1880

It is not merely cruelty that leads (some) men to love war, it is excitement.
>—Henry Ward Beecher, minister,
>*Proverbs from Plymouth Pulpit,* 1887

The Authentic *Budo* Master

Selecting a martial teacher or master is a life-or-death decision. It should, but seldom does, keep one up nights. After all, the life or death held on the balance of surprise is one's own. True believers and skeptics do not recognize this, as the matter is already settled. Their martial art is the ultimate, or they have learned to appreciate booby traps and firepower. For those less burdened by faith, who are sympathetic and uncommitted, the choice is more difficult. Real human beings desire to think for themselves. It is our birthright, at least in most modern democracies. And yet far too many of us have a strong desire (and need) to seek someone who knows more than we do: a leader, a master, a guide through the obscure dangers of combat, a teacher skilled in the business of living who will also help us find the meaning of life. For reasons known best to the seeker, some look to *budo* for such answers.

In the Chinese and Japanese martial arts there are two primary traditions regarding the treatment of a guru or founder. Buddhists expect the founder to be imitated and revered, and followers emulate his or her behavior as much as they are capable of, to a fanatical degree. This "religious" attitude is very popular among masters who have ego deficiencies and followers who are even more desirous or needing of selflessness.

Taoism tradition is more accepting of the frailties of the master but has the expectation that true masters are indifferent to the ways of society and find ambition, knowledge, and religion equally uninteresting, because they have supposedly transcended those definitions from their culture's perspective. Traditional Taoist martial arts masters know the meaning of liberation and have complete freedom to change themselves or the art they teach. Hatsumi-soke seems closer to the Taoist than the Buddhist model. Zen for the most part was less acceptable to the ancient samurai than *mikkyo*, as it developed a form of spiritual creativity that was universal, like the Tao. Spend a moment thinking about Zen practitioners, and then *samurai,* and compare possible outcomes. One finds the older militaristic

Buddhist movements, such as *tendai, shingon,* and *mikkyo* more distant from the unruly *shinto.* Risk analysis can be a good thing.

The concept of Grandmaster is not well understood or embodied by American or Korean martial artists. Both seem to associate the title with achieving a particular rank, rather than heading a lineage. Most American masters are masters of a limited system of techniques, partially derived from an older Japanese or Chinese system, with little interest beyond what they were told or taught. Length of service seldom correlates with depth of knowledge but hopefully indicates technical competence. Mastery is something more than technical knowledge of the forms. True mastery is formless in that the forms are absorbed into the natural movement. In *ninpo,* where the master is a spy, formlessness is the mark of mastery and very few attain it. I have experienced the feeling and have been able to teach it to others, but am too lazy to sustain it like some of my friends that teach martial arts for a living. I am a lucky man, as strange *drala* (Tibetan term for archetypal spirit entities) find me fun to play with and accompany.

Although Musashi was most renowned as a duelist in his own time, his forte in his own opinion was art and strategy *(heiho),* not swordsmanship *(kenjutsu).* He won his most famous duels by surprising tactics, not force of arms. He was a shrewd judge of the shadow and able to shake the confidence of those who attacked or challenged him. As he grew older he often used the appearance of age, fright, or ineptitude to lure a young killer into range. He established a *kenjutsu ryu* that still exists today to test the mettle of those who follow the sword. I have seen Hatsumi-soke show techniques that Takamatsu-soke said were from the Musashi *ryu.* I won't describe them. They are too precious for me to put in a mass-market book. When the Boss was showing *bokken* versus sword to his *shihan* one chilly February night in Kashiwa, many of us were laughing at the unexpectedness of the techniques and thought they originated with Hatsumi-soke. When I suggested that a particularly amusing and unnerving technique made me think of Musashi, his jaw dropped and he said that was exactly where it came from.

There is a Taoist saying, "When everyone knows the good. . . . It is not good." This is a warning concerning how conventionality can cripple creativity as well as keep the naive from looking too closely at the bearer of light, thus missing the shadow. The Taoist understood that the Prophet looked better at a distance, forecasting Tom Wolfe's commentary on the value of distance in enhancing an artist's reputation for holding the "mystagogical compound."

Leon Drucker, a well-known *taiji* and Chinese martial arts instructor in New England, has spent a good many years bumping skulls with some of the best martial artists in the United States and wrote a short story concerning a trip to Japan. I think it fits nicely here:

Last year I was very fortunate to visit Japan for the first time. For most of us, the three thousand dollars or so to make such a trip takes years of saving and planning, and usually something comes up which takes precedence. This time I had the money and, come hell or high water, I was going. I was very lucky to be going with my close friend and instructor Greg Kowalski. Greg had lived in Japan for four years and studied with *soke* and the other *shihan* and speaks fluent Japanese.

At the very least I thought his skills would get us from *dojo* to *dojo*. As it turned out it did much more than that. We wound up staying at Muramatsu-sensei's house! Here is a guy that I would cut off my left arm to train with, and he was letting us stay with him. We had planned our visit to be able to go to the once a year *budo* festival in Meiji Park. This event brought out every martial art including the Zen Archers on horse back! It was a drizzly day but we were not going to let a little rain ruin this very special event. During the morning Greg introduced Muramatsu-sensei to a little old lady about four feet tall. She was, we found out from Greg, a teacher of *naginata-do*. After meeting her, Muramatsu-sensei said that she was a "treasure."

Anyway, during the course of the day this *shihan* of *naginata* was to demo along with her class. The demo was awesome and obviously everybody who could recognize what they saw was really impressed. As this tiny lady made her way back out of the demo area, who out of all the countless martial artists would appear with umbrella in hand but Muramatsu-sensei. As he offered her his umbrella, he got down on his knees in the wet grass and wiped her feet off with a towel so she could put her feet clean and dry into her slippers! I looked over at Greg, who was wiping tears from his eyes and understood the true meaning of the term warrior. For me this was one of the highlights of this trip and certainly an important lesson to remember.

Philosopher-King or Shepherd of Sublime Strategy?

Plato in *The Republic* suggested strongly that the city/state *(poli)* should be ruled by a philosopher-king. In terms of modern and historical organizations this desired state of benevolent rule has seldom actually occurred, and most examples are recent and American. Hatsumi-soke says the *shidoshi* must not lose his "kindness," meaning compassion is an important characteristic of the warrior. Given a choice between compassion and competence, however, the warrior will astutely elect for competence, while the artist may go for compassion. This is an area where the heart may mislead the head and vice versa.

Too often in the teaching and sportification of a martial art it is forgotten that the art was originally created to eradicate the threat of violent confrontation by training the warrior mentally, physically, and spiritually to skillfully protect one's self and loved ones by destroying the enemy or attacker. Sportification and the teaching of children forces the instructor to modify a combat system, removing the deadly aspects and often substituting athletic or aesthetically pleasing substitutes to reduce the risk to the practitioners. Due to legal liability and the popularity of sport systems in the United States, there are very few schools of actual combat.

Often the instructors do not realize they are teaching a watered-down version of what was originally a combat system, because what they have works pretty well until they step out of their home *dojo* or run into someone who has a better system. Your first warning is strong tendency by the "philosopher kings" to regard their art as the ultimate with there being no need to study elsewhere. This is even more amusing when weapons, particularly modern weapons, are not taught. There is a tremendous emphasis on being the good guys without taking into consideration what the bad boys consider to be ultimate training or practice. When the good guys won't lower themselves to practice against the bad guys because they (the bad guys) have no sense of morality or ethics, it is almost guaranteed that you are being set up for a very rugged experience in survival by a Shepherd of Sublime Strategy. As the coffee mug of divination states, "Treachery and experience defeats enthusiasm and innocence."

In the teaching of some schools of *jujutsu* there has been a movement away from the teaching of the brutal combat techniques in favor of moving to a more *aikido*-like presentation of the art in order to assuage the worries of the "soccer moms" and reduce the liabilities of owning a school. *Aikido*ists forget that the Osensei was a butcher in Manchuria *(Manchuko)* and became a martial saint in his middle years. Even *bujinkan* has undergone experimentation with removing some of the more brutal training techniques from the *kihon* (basic stuff). This has reduced the rate of blown-out shoulders and broken legs in the overconfident and muscle-reliant. These changes have not been greeted with enthusiasm by some of the grayer wolves in the hierarchy. Some of the older fighters have severed relationships with the *hombu* over this and continue to teach in the manner to which they are accustomed. Others have become distant because they do not want to learn the new system (and go back to white belt). Others have never really accepted their proper role in *bujinden,* and use this as an excuse to justify their inability to work with others. Although I agree in general with Hatsumi-soke's philosophy of creating a more trainee-friendly *bujinkan,* it is important that the initiates understand that this is *taisabaki* (movement training) and the really nasty applications and variations *(henke)* will be slipped back in during their *dan* years when they attend seminars and *tai kai.* For most of us the new is only slightly less effective than the old, and still will terrify, as well as challenge the thinking neophyte.

The Sword-of-Justice Syndrome

Revenge is the more practiced word in the West, but the concept of knighthood holds a strong attraction for the average martial artist. Serving virtue by eradicating evil is normally thought of as police work. If you have the urge to while away the hours by hanging out in the bad parts of town so you can collect a few scalps in self-defense to decorate the *dojo* attic or inner sanctum, remember that vigilantism is frowned upon by the legal system. It is not considered cricket to haunt the subways with a stone knife or .380, even when the blood calls and the police are busy writing traffic tickets.

Livereatin' Johnson (one of my all-time personal American heroes next to Abe Lincoln and Crazy Horse) set off a cycle of vengeance by his just treatment of his attackers. Justice has a lot to do with your sense of irony and history or with which side is telling the story. The *samurai* were hardly the only honorable people who lived in Japan, just as WASPS were hardly the only settlers in North America worthy of being included in history books. For an eye-opener, study up on the Iroquois and Seneca. Smart people.

Asians like their vengeance served cold, often long after the original insult has been forgotten. (For most Americans the best revenge is living well.) When one picks up the sword of justice it feels heroic, but in Western tradition it is good to remember a favorite theme of mythology: those that the gods wish to punish they first make proud, then crazy. Romeo and Juliet, the Earps and Clantons of Tombstone fame, as well as the Hatfields and McCoys' Appalachian adventures are all a reminder that once the blood begins to flow there is no telling how long, until, or where it will stop. "Vengeance is mine! Thus saeth the Lord." Americans are told, "When you take up the gun for vengeance, dig an extra grave for yourself."

There are times when the law is corrupted by money and power or is too distant to create or preserve gentility. It is at those times you have to assume the mantle of natural justice. Your training in *hieho* may be all that can sustain you in the dark. You will find it easier to select individual targets over organizations, because the snake does not function well without its head. Subtle influence can have many levels of meaning, and a master of *budo* is responsible for creating an environment where loving hearts may flourish. This part of the secret oral tradition of many otherwise legal societies is usually followed by the admonition, "Don't get caught! You are on your own."

The Master-of-the-Game Syndrome

The Brits love the gaming mentality. There is an awful little book that was published back in the late fifties or early sixties titled *One-upmanship: How to Win Without Actually Cheating.* It's a book of strategies for dealing with the pathologies of everyday life when you don't have the upper hand and need more power. It was my Musashi when I was a freshman in college. My tastes are less Machiavellian now, so I won't give you more than the above about the book, but it can be very useful if you have the will to intimidate.

Trapping others is a form of inflating the ego that is great fun. The trapper gets to feel more clever than the trappee. It's a basic theme in most spy thrillers. Playing Dungeons & Dragons or other fun role-playing games can teach one how to build believable scenarios. The Prussian high command developed gaming to train officers for real warfare and the American OSS used the techniques to develop spies for World War II. I used role-playing games to teach my children achievement motivation and my college students strategy. Because we changed the dungeon master with great regularity, one was never sure who was the better teacher. In *bujinkan* some of the best sword techniques come out of offering a weakness to the skilled opponent, then taking it away when he or she commits. Hatsumi-soke sometimes attempts to create ego-deflation through the awarding of inappropriate rank. To the Japanese this is a common strategy used to make the person awarded the high rank wake up and stop posturing. However, it doesn't work very well with

Americans, as most aren't aware of the tradition or refuse to face their condition.

The gaming mentality works best when the others don't realize you are gaming. It becomes painful when the game or role becomes more important than developing a real or authentic relationship.

The Good Helper and Source of Special Knowledge

"I am here to help you" is not just an IRS slogan. Some teachers see themselves as helpers and often create dependence, because they are the ones who come up with the solutions. A student will do better in the long run if he or she does not become overly dependent on the goodwill and experience of the *sensei* but continues to study on his or her own. The best teachers create skilled spontaneity, not masterful imitation. Discovery is still the best way to learn because it forces one into a primal mental state of no expectations.

Many teachers become overly reliant on having a good *uke* so they can showcase their skills to best advantage. Your *uke* should not matter in terms of showing yourself off. The *uke* should be capable of surviving what you are doing without damage, and you should be controlled enough not to injure the poor bastard seriously or question your mastery. A good *uke* is worth his or her weight in gold when you are the star of a demo, and when you are training, a bad *uke* helps you find your weaknesses. When you take the title of master you should be able to handle whatever the *uke* brings into play.

In training it should be recognized that the object of getting together is to learn technique, not defeat your training partner. Most seminar attendees are pretty skilled at something, or very curious about the teacher, or they wouldn't take the risk. Give them respect, not a bad time. If you confidently treat the wrong person badly as an *uke*, he or she might give you a taste of what has occupied their training.

In *hoshin*, and with some of the *ninja* masters, it is the *uke*'s responsibility to share his or her fears with the master so that situations can be created that force he or she to overcome that fear and continue with the play. Going through a situation that would normally reduce you to pants-wetting terror in the company of someone you trust to be able to rescue you is stressful but often results in real growth. Fire-walking is a small example of this type of training. For me it is attending some psychopath's seminar and surviving. Millis-shihan could usually get my blood cold and adrenals cooking.

The Virtuous-Leader Syndrome

Aikido and *judo* players tend to fall more often than not into this category. Morihei Ueshiba and Jigaro Kano are generally recognized as *budo* immortals, representing what is most positive in the martial arts. Most of the modern players tend to forget that Kano-san spent years being brutally tossed about in various *jujutsu* schools before figuring out how to teach the art in a safer way to schoolchildren and police, coming up with *judo*. The founder of *aikido* saw himself as a *shinto* demigod (and was probably right) and *aikido* was his religious form of *budo*.

Too often the modern teachers of these arts begin to believe there is a morality to their art because they perceive it to be essentially defensive. Goody-goodies get eaten if they can't out-think the baddy-baddies. I have always thought the Detroit *bujinkan's* motto was terribly appropriate, given the competition lurking in the environment: "We eat the weak."

Virtue is decided by social expectation, and those virtues that are attached to *budo,* interestingly enough, relate to harmony, calm, wisdom, neutrality, and truth, as opposed to good or bad. Spirituality is the direct personal relationship with the Tao, but religion is a social construct that may or may not have any relationship to spirituality. From that perspective we are all the good guys. *Budo* should lead one to respond rather than react.

Our spiritual problems are not very different from those of our ancestors. Today's search for truth often leads to that place within us that has always existed latently, unbroken and eternal, discussed by the Taoist masters, mystics of many stripes, shamans, and European alchemists. When one has an experience of transcendence on the order of the kundalini, or gradually develops a relationship with the Tao, the need for religion as a social construct evaporates. When *mushin* is achieved, religion appears as a mild form of lunacy used to promote proactive social behavior in those who can't figure out how to get along (like the Lotto as taxes for those who can't grasp statistics). For the transcendent to try to become a religious leader is only to repeat the mistakes of countless other genuine seekers.

The Dangers of Leading

Do you really know where you are going? A little good can draw one to evil, just as a lot of evil can lead to the pursuit of good. One often leads when one should follow. Too often people find or look for a weakness so they can denigrate the whole. It must be remembered that a woody has no conscience, particularly in that place where there is no good or bad or right or wrong. Real leaders are aware of their weaknesses and use them as part of their strategies.

Concerning Enlightened Consciousness

Be great-hearted, my friend.
Like Athos and the kings of old.
Torn with the pangs of love?
Yearning for true soul in your very blood?
That is your lot, I'm afraid,
As a man of passion.
But perhaps at later time, on another day,
You'll realize what this life really means,
And you'll feel exquisite joy in the midst of your pain,
And savor your sorrows,
And recognize the inherent tragedy of life
While still remaining cheerful, and *know*

how life's tragedy is its very meaning, its only true joy.
Yes, my friend, these lessons you will learn,
At the cost of innocence, perhaps,
And you will lose your grandiose self-importance,
And see the world as it truly is, and yourself as you truly are.
Great-hearted as a man who has seen much,
And noble as one who realizes his place in the universe,
You will claim your prize for emerging from Ignorance:
Freedom and Truth, and though you will have lost some
    happiness,
You will have Serenity.

—Anuragh Mehta

CHAPTER SIX

Exercises to Increase Chi

*Les méchants sont toujours surpris de trouver de
l'habileté dans le bons. (The wicked are always
surprised to find ability in the good.)*
—Marquis de Vauvenargues, nobleman,
Réflexions et maximes, 1746

Among the great things which are to be among us, the Being
of Nothingness is the greatest.
Leonardo de Vinci, architect, artilleryman,
artist, sculptor, inventor, grave robber,
Leonardo Da Vinci's Notebooks, Sixteenth century

The danger is not that a particular class is unfit to govern.
Every class is unfit to govern.
Lord Acton, politician,
letter to Mary Gladstone, 1881

Describing the Air in the Air

In the twelve years since I began chronicling the effects of *chi kung* training on martial artists from a psychological perspective, I've received a lot of letters asking how I actually teach what I have experienced. I've acquired a few hundred students; some actually wanted to teach from my perspective and became *deshi*. My concept of *deshi* is pretty loose, but it can be said that I try to teach them the stuff as I understand it, and they in turn are able to make it their own. This chapter is in their words; they are describing some techniques they found useful.

Ken and Becca's Energy Medicine

Ken Morgan and Rebecca (Becca) Robertson are healers that work and play in Lake Charles, Louisiana. They are more concerned with healing than breaking—a much saner viewpoint than most of my students have. They teach the *hoshintao chi kung* system (*hoshintao* being a word I invented to describe their unique blend of healing/meditative practices). Robin Martin is a fifth *dan* in *hoshin*, is *dan* ranked in other arts, and heads the *shinjinkan dojo* in Lake Charles. Wayne Oliver is a product of Robin and myself who also studies with Greg Kowalski. Wayne owns Madrigal Investigations and is a graduate student in graphic arts who designed the cover of *Shadow Strategies*. He is a private investigator in New Orleans and Lake Charles and is very good at finding people who don't want to be found. What follows is from these students' perspectives.

Chi kung (qigong) is the science of bioelectrical energy generation/cultivation and circulation within the human body. The result of *chi kung* practice is increased physical and mental health and vitality. *Chi kung* is an ancient practice that has been used by the Chinese for thousands of years. One learns to direct this energy (called *chi*) by the intent of will through the use of the breath, as in some Indian yogic practices.

Chi kung training is divided into two main categories: martial *chi kung* (dealing with the combative arts) and pure *chi kung* for increased health, longevity, and spiritual attainment. The practice of *hoshintao* deals with both forms.

Hoshintao chi kung focuses on opening the chakra and kundalini channels through the combination of a medical system (called in Chinese *taotien,* or heaven way) and a military system (called in Japanese *hoshin,* or true spirit). Medical systems emphasize health and longevity, where military systems stress speed, power, and harmony. There are meditation, visualization, and physical techniques appropriate to the healer, yoga practitioner, and martial artist. The practitioner of *hoshintao* will learn the theories and principles of *chi kung* and be able to bring its benefits into every facet of life. Chinese medicine emphasizes balancing and strengthening the body so that it can heal itself. The practice of these techniques allowed Dr. Morris to reverse the effects of arthritis within his own body almost ten years ago. In 1985, Dr. Morris achieved the rising of the kundalini (greater *kan* and *li*) using these techniques. Since then he has been able to guide over forty of his students toward successful and relatively painless kundalini awakenings.

In *hoshintao* (way of the true spirit/warrior heart) *chi kung,* we learn to master meditative practices that increase and refine the inner energies of the body and also learn how those energies can be used in self-defense. Developing this inner (spiritual) strength is the true secret of the enlightened martial artist, as reflected in the legendary Shaolin monks of China. In sharing his teachings, Dr. Morris has encouraged us to go share this wisdom with others. As instructors of *hoshintao,* we are able to focus on opening and balancing the body's energy centers (chakra), as well as the physical movements, postures, and defensive techniques associated with each center. We have found that the highest levels of mastery in martial arts were often achieved by those who focused on developing and refining the spiritual side of themselves as well as the physical side. As the name *hoshintao* implies, we seek to balance and integrate both sides in order to become better, more complete human beings. In doing so, we may even reach enlightenment.

The purpose of *chi kung* is the attempt by the practitioner to consolidate the health of the body, breath, and mind. However, the practitioner considers all three of these to be one, for what occurs in the physical is reflected in the breath, spirit, and mind. *The body knows better than the mind* what it needs and likes to be healthy. This is true in the pure *chi kung* practices as well as the martial aspects of training.

Taoist *chi kung* involved the extensive use of three substances produced or used by the body. These materials came to be known as the Three Treasures. The ancient Chinese internal alchemists described and cataloged the Three Treasures in three categories.

Jing: The *jing* involves the male sperm or female hormones, chemicals, the entire endocrine system, and genetic makeup. It is what makes a person what they are. Sperm is empowered by the *chi* and travels within the spine to feed the body and brain with its nutrient-rich makeup. In the female, hormones from the ovaries and other organs sustain this function. *Chi kung* skills allow sperm energy and hormones to be transported where needed.

Chi: Chi is the energy of life, life essence, and breath. (These are almost literal translations of the term.) This is the aspect that is most heavily focused on by the practice of *hoshintao chi kung*. *Chi* is the material in the universe that keeps us alive. We breathe *chi* when we inhale, consume *chi* when we eat, and use *chi* in healing and in combat. The *chi* that is most easily worked is derived from sexual energy or *jing*. (This has been true for everyone I've ever worked with. *Jing* is the most basic and powerful creative energy, and easiest to feel.)

Shen: The *shen (shin)* is the energy in the mind (thought of as higher *chi* or transmuted *chi*). In later practices and higher exercises in *chi kung* training, the *chi* can be transformed into *shen*. It is said that this process is what leads to enlightenment. We have two theories as to what happens: The first is that through the practice of meditation, the production and circulation of *chi* grows until at some point it transforms into *shen* and races up the spine to result in the kundalini energy. The other is that the actual process of kundalini changes the *chi* into *shen*. Or perhaps the *chi* cannot be transmuted into *shen* until the kundalini or its equivalent occurs, because the kundalini does not always yield *satori* (bliss).

Jing is thought to determine most of that which is physical. The Taoists believed that *jing* was finite and could be easily diminished by illness, overwork, stress, poor nutrition, lack of sleep, or the use of drugs. However, lost *jing* can be replaced by proper diet and energy work. *Jing* begins in the feet.

Humans are born with a certain amount of *chi* inherited from their parents. From there, the child must begin to gather his or her own *chi* through breathing. Because *chi* is so closely associated with breath (except at the highest levels), it is clearly married to blood circulation, oxygen, and the nerve impulses. Strong *chi,* it is said, strengthens the immune system, increases stamina, and aids in longevity. *Chi* circulates through the blood by traveling within the oxygen and through invisible paths in the body known in Chinese medicine as meridians, where the *chi* makes use of the tissues to go where it is needed. Meridians are energy channels that cannot be found through the dissection of human specimens. Ancient *chi kung* practitioners were made aware of their existence by the use of introspective meditation. They looked inside their own bodies to see and feel what was going on and experimented with cause and effect. In this manner they compared the body to the universe, seeing it as a microcosm of all that was around them. They reasoned that because the universe is in constant motion, there must be a similar motion within the body.

The ancient Chinese found these paths of motion and mapped them. Meridians are not tubes through which the bioelectrical energy travels, but are patterns of energy flow within the body. When meridians are blocked (due to illness, stress, injury, or poor diet) an imbalance occurs within the body that results in health problems in either the area of the blockage or throughout the whole corresponding system. Sometimes a blockage will result in the efficiency of an organ being reduced or impaired. Many imbalances can be corrected by various *hoshintao* techniques.

Robin Martin's Visualizations

Robin Martin has developed a side practice of teaching *chi kung* meditation to massage therapists as well as integrating it into his teaching of *jujutsu*. Following are some of his favorite meditation techniques. His *dojo* is *shinjinkan* (School for the Human Spirit) in Lake Charles, Louisiana, and is a division of Defense Technologies. His variation of *hoshin* and *danzan jujutsu* has resulted in some of the scariest throwing techniques I've seen. Here are his techniques (geared for the teacher, this time, rather than the student) in his own words, with my comments in smaller type.

1. Nine Gates, or Nine Elders

Note: This can be used to deepen a trance or to relax a student to the point of sleep. Do not be surprised to hear Tibetan buzzsaw mantras.

Practitioner should be lying on back, legs slightly apart, toes relaxed and falling outward. Arms are slightly away from the side, with palms facing up similar to the yogic deadman position. Fingers may seek mudra appropriate to the level, or chakra, you are working on.

Level 1. Begin by breathing slowly and deeply filling the chest and abdomen as fully as possible. Students should visualize that they are totally filling and emptying the lungs and stomach. Tell them to try for 100 percent exchange of air. Do this three times.

Level 2. Continue breathing, but lower inhalation and exhalation to 75 percent of chest and abdomen capacity. Do this three times.

Level 3. Continue breathing, but lower inhalation and exhalation to 50 percent of chest and abdomen capacity. Do this three times.

Level 4. Continue breathing, but lower inhalation and exhalation to 50 percent of chest and abdomen capacity. Do this three times.

Level 5. Continue breathing, but lower inhalation and exhalation to 75 percent of chest and abdomen capacity. Do this three times.

Level 6. Continue breathing, but lower inhalation and exhalation to 100 percent of chest and abdomen capacity. Do this three times.

A total of eighteen breaths are performed as slowly and deeply as possible. Body and mind become very relaxed and very oxygenated. Now the students can go on a real voyage to the undiscovered country within.

2. White Light or Laser Light

Note: Student needs to be able to breath through his or her crown chakra, an advanced exercise.

Begin with deep breathing, drawing in through your crown chakra while listening to "space" music (something like *Mysterious Void*). Once sufficiently relaxed and deep enough, attempt to open your chakras. Those that are clear will open easily, while those that are blocked will benefit from this and be blown open by the light.

Visualize your body as a vast empty chamber, or perhaps the insides of a giant statute of yourself. I like to see myself as sitting in a lotus position, like a Buddha would. Bring the white light from the universe down through the crown of your head as if you had opened just a peephole and a single shaft of pure white light is penetrating the darkness of your body. Watch as the dust motes dance in the light. If there are any unfriendlies in the shadows, send them scampering away in fear of this light's cleansing effects. Let this light shine on your tailbone and slowly warm it up. As it heats up it will slowly open like a flower.

> The ancient Vedic and tantric texts of India use a similar process to Robin's but put a heavier emphasis on the sexual organs. When you enter "tantric country" there are many huge statues of *lingum* and *yoni* (male and female sex organs in rampant display, rather like the Washington Monument, but not so tall and pointy) dotting the hillsides. This motif can also be used in meditation as part of one's visualizations. I've had male student meditators spontaneously make comments like, "I see my

energy as a penis becoming erect; it helps open my root chakra. At least that is where I feel it anyway, so there is nothing kinky about it." I suspect this is another universal power-building image available to the skilled meditator. For some people, particularly Americans, the sexual symbolism in meditation can be quite graphic. The flower can symbolize chakras of either male or female sex organs.

Inside the flower is a mirror. Once the beam of light strikes the mirror, it lances out towards my first chakra, the root. It burns through the root chakra and punches out to light the air in front of my groin. If the root is blocked, the light opens it by burning away the blockage. I feel a sudden release of pressure and anxiety. It's a pleasant, almost sexual sensation.

The ancient tantrics would use a drop of semen instead of a mirror. The light hits and reflects off it, doing the same thing as the mirror.

As the flower continues to raise its head, the mirror tilts upward to each chakra, burning through them just as it did the root. I open the root, navel, solar plexus, throat, one on the roof of my mouth, third eye, fifth eye, and at the hair line. Once these are all open I turn to my spine.

I look for blockages in my spine and let the mirror turn toward them and burn them away. Then I search for other problems, and again the light sears them into nothing. Slowly, bit by bit, I punch so many holes in my outer shell that there is no longer any me, there is only open air filled with intense pure white light. The problems, blockages, pain, and doubt are gone, burned up by the power of the universe.

Students should expect to see wild sights with this, feel rushes of power, and may experience a rising of kundalini energy. They may or may not experience the complete rising, but they may see snakes, dragons, goddesses, and other symbols of higher consciousness. They may also experience states of bliss for some time after the meditation—a euphoric high.

3. Healing Meditation

This exercise is good for relaxation before a massage or as a standard meditation in the *hoshin* repertoire. Start students breathing deeply with proper music in the background. Take them through a guided relaxation exercise with the breathing until you see them begin to relax in the shoulders and neck. Then suggest that they visualize that they are at the top of a flight of ten steps. The steps lead down into the darkness, and they are not afraid. Have them visualize stepping off with the left foot first, feeling their weight sink onto the step as their foot touches down. Have them time the steps with their slow breathing. Take your time and do all ten steps. As they descend they get more and more relaxed and heavier. When they are sufficiently relaxed, begin this guided meditation:

> When you reach the bottom of the steps the darkness clears away and you are facing a great flat plain, which disappears into the distance. A few yards away is a door unsupported by any walls. It just hangs there in the air. You go to the door and open it to another dimension. Inside and beyond is a large room with walls, floor, and ceiling. The wall directly across from you is made entirely of a giant television screen. Before it is a recliner. The recliner is in the center of the floor. You walk over to the recliner, sit, and lean back.
>
> The television comes on. You watch yourself as a bird, soaring over great expanses of earth. (I let them choose the terrain. I am often surprised at the difference in terrain people come up with, but it's all personal preference.) As you watch the television, the chair vibrates you, relaxing your muscles. Soon you become so relaxed that you turn to jelly.
>
> You become a gelatinous mass that slowly begins to seep through the chair to the floor below. The floor below is a large

sieve, like a filter. You slowly seep through the filter to a room below. As you soften and melt, you leave on top of the screen lumps of problems, unresolved issues, and aches and pains accumulated during the day. These all stay on top.

Meanwhile, below, you are dripping into a hammered gold mold of yourself. As you are pooling in this mold you appear to be gold and viscous like honey. There is no blemish, sore, pimple, or bruise on this new body. Your mind is clear and has nothing to cloud your thinking or make you feel depressed or angry. Everything troubling remains above on the filter. (It works best to draw this melting out over a good length of time. Have them drop through one drippy drop at a time. Make oozing a very lengthy process. Get rid of everything. Once they are fully reformed, with none the bad stuff remaining, have them sit up in the mold.)

In front of you at the foot of the mold is a mirror. In the mirror, see yourself healed, renewed, cleansed of everything that holds you back or distracts you from your goal(s). (Let them marvel at themselves in the mirror for awhile.) You climb out of the mold and move lithely to a shimmering door. You open the door, and it looks out on a beautiful white-sand beach.

You can walk or jog along the beach. Enjoy the wind, the sun, the sand, and the waves. Exhilarate in the occasion, its freedom and release. Feel alive and excited to be so free.

Sit on the sand and relax. Lie back and bask in the sun. The sun heats up your new body and you slowly melt into the sand. You become one with the earth. You feel the movement of the sand, animals, bugs, etc. You become smaller and finer, and eventually the sand becomes larger and larger. From its minute size it grows to that of rocks, then boulders. Finally it is the size of planets, and you are slowly, gracefully, falling like a feather between the great cosmic-sized grains of sand. You are falling toward a bright pinpoint of light far below.

As you fall toward the light, you see it become slowly larger and larger. The light is our sun. As you approach it you feel its heat as a welcome and friendly warmth. It grows and grows and you pass harmlessly right through it. It feels like a hot shower that cleanses you and makes you even more radiant and pure. (Every time they fall through something, make them better, cleaner, healthier.) As you fall past the sun you see the beautiful blue ball of Earth below. You fall toward Earth slowly, floating like a dust mote, and see yourself sitting in the room where you started the meditation. You are a minute piece of energy, smaller than an atom. You float down (to a point just above whichever chakra you are working) and enter the body (through that opening). Slowly you fill yourself up with this clean, pure energy. You recharge yourself. You feel invigorated and renewed. Take a moment and pay attention to how your body feels. When you are ready, allow yourself to open your eyes and savor the moment.

Those are three of my favorites. They always seem to work well for me and my students. Use a deep, calming voice with proper mood music and they'll drop like pennies in a well.

Dr. Death's Spider Stretches

When you go to meet the goddess in meditation, you should prepare yourself as if for a wedding. The positions *(asanas)* in yoga that conceal hidden *kamae* (martial arts postures used in fighting) are the warrior poses. If you loosen up to meditate by doing the *asanas* very slowly, particularly the one-footed stances, and allow yourself to contract with fear before expanding into power, you may find what has been hidden by the yin warriors, as women need protection as well as effective retaliation. Energy often blocks between the shoulder blades, base of the skull, and small of the back. Good posture, exercising the lats, and opening your neck and upper body by throwing your chest forward while spreading out your arms and fingers at different levels in imitation of a many-armed statue of *kali* will increase your ease.

CHAPTER SEVEN

Exercises Linking Intuition to Action

Wrong must not win by technicalities.
—Aeschylus, philosopher, *Euminedes*, 458 B.C.E.

This court will not deny the equal protection of the law to the unwashed, unshod, unkempt, and uninhibited.
—Herman Weinkrantz, judge,
ruling on harassment of hippies, 1968

Oppression makes a wise man mad.
—Frederick Douglass, orator and abolitionist,
speech, 1852

Intuition: Trusting Your Feelings

Ninpo and some forms of *jujitsu* emphasize techniques that involve developing creativity and intuition, not just focusing on technical perfection. The student learns more quickly at a subconscious level and the doorway is left open for a certain amount of creativity to creep into the methodology.

Working with the emotions and being in touch with one's feelings while interpreting the "feel" of others results in the student developing what looks like mind-reading abilities or *tashinjitsu.*. One begins to react to the feeling without thought, because feelings or intentions come before actual thought and action.

Lonie Hilton is a *bujinkan* teacher in Don Mills, a suburb of Toronto, who uses animal imagery to teach techniques. His students play at being monkeys. A visit to the zoo can be helpful for those who have never taken the time to really watch nonhuman primates. It's amazing how quickly one can learn to roll around and move with full body attention when one has the right animal model to observe. Not being as flexible as Lonie, I use the bear and gorilla more. In *shing yi (hsing-i)*, a Chinese martial art, specific animals represent chakras and the fighting postures. Some *chi kung* forms, like the five-animal frolics, increase a practitioner's strength and mobility of energy use. I have seen them taught in a very serious and meticulous manner, indicating the teacher had forgotten what the word "frolic" is all about. (I like to call them the horn, fang, toothies, hoofies, claws, and beaked critter frolics.) It is more important to assume the *attitude* of the animal than to imitate its movement: How would a bear deal with this situation? The bear moves its paw like this.

Leo Langwith, a *ninpo* practitioner (a *shodan* in *hoshin* as well as a student of *bujinkan*), teaches excellent self-defense techniques in Ann Arbor, Michigan (from a very heady perspective), using the following attitudes to teach his students to deal with realistic fight scenarios:

Uke has contempt for you and is going to kick your ass into the next county.

Uke is afraid of you but is going to attack you anyway.

Uke regards you as a challenge to show off his martial skills.

Uke is drunk and thinks his woman is trying to pick you up.

Uke thinks you are attractive and is going to have his way with you.

Uke is your loutish brother-in-law who wants to whip you out of jealousy.

Uke is a power lifter who wants to teach you what he learned from his buddies in prison (the ones who would rather hear a fat boy fart than see a pretty girl stretch).

Try assuming each of these attitudes while you are sparring or learning a new technique and you may be greatly surprised at how they will change the fight scenario. This is almost as much fun as adding different types of weapons.

Leon Goltsman is a *sandan* in *shotokan* good enough to be selected for the Israeli Macabiah Games, he ranked second in the *shotokan* world at *kata*, studied *hoshin* and attended all my seminars when I was in Australia working with Geoff Smith, and opened the first *hoshin dojo* in Sydney. Being a typical hard *karateka*, Leon found what I taught (trusting one's feelings to enhance avoidance techniques) quite amazing and intriguing. He really worked hard at it—more so than the other *shotokan* instructors who attended and were more interested in showing their own stuff.

A few weeks later at the Games' opening at Ramut Gan Stadium, the Australian contingent of 380 athletes led the march into the stadium across a forty-eight-foot-high bridge. Two died and sixty-four were injured, seven seriously, as the bridge collapsed, hurling dozens of athletes into the river below. Leon had had a "bad feeling" and stepped back when the others moved forward. *Saaki.* He then joined with one of the rugby teams to help rescue people. Leon is a fine human being and represents both himself and the martial arts in general as an example of how the study of *budo* can refine and make an individual more gentle.

Below is a pure-energy exercise from the *hoshintao chi kung* to speed the beneficial process of intuitive development.

Cosmic Energy Micro Orbit

This *chi* exercise, known as the Gathering of the Original, was adapted by Wayne Oliver. This meditation should be performed while you are sitting in a chair. This is a complex and involved meditation with many steps, but it moves energy powerfully and balances flow of energy within the body. It is well worth mastering, but it should not be attempted at the lower levels of practice.

1. Begin Buddha breathing. Calm the mind, pulse, spirit, and breath. Close your eyes.

2. Open each of the basic chakras in the body according to color and feel, beginning with the root chakra.

3. Bring your attention to the *tantien* (small intestines) until you begin to feel the warmth in that area (two inches below the navel and about one and a half inches within the belly). Concentrate on this area for approximately thirty-six breaths, collecting the *chi* here.

4. Once the navel is warm and you have collected the *chi* into the *tantien,* condense it into a ball, making it smaller and smaller until it is a tiny dot within the *tantien.* This should take about nine breaths.

5. Relax and expand the ball into a glowing sun about five inches in diameter.

6. Perform spinal breathing. Draw *chi* into the spine and down into the root chakra, creating a second ball. Do this for nine breaths.

7. Draw the second ball of *chi* down and up the front of the body until it merges with the first ball.

8. Bang the teeth together nine times and swirl the tongue around the mouth to gather saliva. When you have a good amount, swallow it, following its path to the *tantien* with your mind's eye. See it mix with the energy ball there.

9. Squeeze and release the rectum nine times in conjunction with the breath.

10. Condense the energy ball once again until it is about the size of a marble.

11. Become aware of a mist of golden smoke or fog that floats right in front of your nose. Inhale this mist into your mouth and begin forming a ball of energy inside of your mouth. Build up this ball with approximately nine breaths, then swallow it down into the *tantien*, where it combines with the ball of energy already there. The two-balls-as-one glow brightly like a golden sun. (The key is to see it golden in color.)

12. Pull this sun-ball down into the *perineum (tain't)*, or base of the spine, where it begins to spin. As the ball spins, it begins to elongate until it becomes a long strand of energy that enters the spine and begins to flow upward (inhale), cleansing the spinal marrow as it proceeds.

13. As you exhale, black, red, sickly green, or gray impurities flow out of the spine with the breath and into the air, out of your body. Repeat this step for at least fifteen cycles of breath, or until the exhalation is pure white in color.

14. Once more begin spinal breathing (at the base, middle, and jade gates) to feed this pulsing energy within the spine. Do this for at least nine breaths.

15. Bring your attention to the third eye. Concentrate on the pulsing purple or indigo energy that resides there until you can feel it. (A traditional way to open the third eye is to touch it and spiral the finger and eyes clockwise. A simpler way is to lightly touch it while sending *chi* out through your index finger into the brain.) Begin to breath into the third eye (inhale gold,

exhale purple) from a large ball of golden energy that floats in front of your third eye. Inhale its energy.

16. With the third eye pulsing, bring your mind to the pulsing energy in the *tantien*. Continue for as many breaths as you can do comfortably.

17. At this point, inhale the entire ball of energy in through your third eye and drop it down into the mouth. Bang your teeth together to fill the mouth with saliva. Mix the saliva with the golden ball and swallow it down, following its path down the front of your body. See the path of golden liquid-light as it flows down the front of your body and rests at the *perineum*. From here you begin to perform the microcosmic orbit. Circulate the golden energy through the micro-cosmic orbit at least nine times.

18. Picture the spine glowing blindingly bright with golden energy that flows up the spine like a fountain. The energy flows all the way up to the crown chakra and to the third eye. Feel this fountain of energy begin to expand into a large pillar of white light, much like the golden light meditation. See it flow out of the confines of your body until it merges with your aura and you are surrounded by a ball of shining energy. Sit within this ball of energy, concentrating simply on your Buddha breathing. Continue to breathe within this ball for as long as you would like, but for at least eighteen cycles of breath.

19. Once again, as with the golden light meditation, pull the energy back into the spine. Feel the fountain one more time. Then draw the fountain up the spine into a ball at the crown chakra. Hold here for a few breaths. Feel it pulse and flow out of the crown chakra. Then inhale it back into the head and push it forward into the third eye. Feel it pulse at the third eye for several breath cycles.

20. Inhale and bring the ball of energy down to the *perineum*. Exhale and push it into the base of the spine. Perform the orbit for at least nine breath cycles.

21. Bring the energy ball to the heart chakra. Inhale and bring more energy through the third eye into the ball, exhaling and contracting it for nine breaths.

22. Draw in cool blue energy from the throat and red energy in through the soles of the feet and up into the ball at the heart. Do this for about twenty breaths.

23. Concentrate on an area above the crown chakra. Take your consciousness up to a point about five feet above your head. Then pull the ball into the spine and exhale all this energy up out of the crown chakra and into this point above your head. Expand this energy ball out into the universe, letting it grow larger with every breath. Feel the stream of energy flowing between you and this point above your head as it expands. Do this for at least thirty-six cycles of breath.

24. Begin to inhale energy from the universe (white) into this ball above your head as you contract it. Make it dense and small with the energy of the universe. Do this for as long as you are comfortable, but limit yourself to small amounts when beginning this practice.

25. Inhale the ball down into the crown and down the front channel. Inhale it into the *tantien*. Continue to inhale a mist of silvery white energy from the universe into the *tantien* for six breaths. Exhale and condense this ball.

26. Inhale, collect all the free floating *chi* within your body into the ball, and store it at the *tantien*.

27. Rub your face and ears. Bang your fingertips over your head and neck. Make sure to do some stretching or light physical activity after this meditation.

This type of exercise, if practiced with care along with sensitivity drills and other fun experiences like hugging trees, fire walking, stalking, and energy work in general, will have amazing effects on your physical skills. If practiced with diligence the result will be an opening the mind. This exercise is on audio tape and is available on the *hoshin* website.

Four-Way Breathing or Reverse Breathing

This is a technique I lifted from Dr. Yang Jwing-Ming. Dr. Yang is a serious practitioner, good natural scientist, and teaches a great seminar. If you really want to be nasty in your particular art, a little time spent with Dr. Yang in the study of White Crane and Eagle Claw *chin-na* will enhance your skills at finger throws and wrist techniques. His Ph.D. is in engineering, so his presentations are humorous and orderly and his understanding of placement and leverage far exceeds the average instructor.

Now, this is my interpretation of his explanation of developing *jing* to enhance one's *chi*. The White Crane practitioner focuses on finding one's center and placing one's breathing on a point somewhere between the *dan tien (hara)* and *ming men* (center of lower back) in the center of the body (the intestines).

The White Crane practitioner puts the emphasis not on the energy orbits but on the *ming men*. Reverse might be better said as backward. As the person breathes in, he or she tightens the stomach muscles, spreads the bottom of the ribs, rocks the hips back, and pushes out the muscles of the lower back. As he or she exhales, he or she relaxes the stomach muscles and pulls in the back, reversing the Buddha breath pattern. The movement massages the kidneys and interestingly quiets tinnitus. This is practiced in a meditative state, then used as one walks around. Its benefits can be enhanced by dancing or jumping about to shake the body. (When I teach reverse breathing, the energy orbits in the body are being reversed to cool the yang energy for a safer kundalini experience.) The White Crane energy flow remains from the genitals up the spine, and is only reversed when making love à la *shing-yi* "happy woman" exercises or *yab-yum* (see *Path Notes*).

Psychic Exercises

Dr. John Porter pioneered fire walking for me when I was a professor at Hillsdale College. He has an interesting counseling practice based on psychometric instruments that I developed to measure *ninja* concepts back in the eighties. We are working on a book of definitions and exercises for those who want to explore the esoteric side of *budo*. His Quest for Personal Growth *dojo* near Cincinnati is a center for intense, unique training experiences. Here are four fun ones you can try out, as well as a bunch more in the next chapter on teaching.

"Catch" is an exercise to build PK (psychokinetic) skills. Two partners blindfold themselves. They begin the exercise by tossing a soft object back and forth. A bean bag is best as it easy to catch. To develop PK, avoid establishing a throwing pattern. Advance versions of the exercise include increasing distance, adding more participants, changing the object thrown (hard and sharp tends to increase attention), and putting one or more blindfolded participants in the path of the throw.

For the "tree game," find a moderately dense irregularly patterned grove of trees. An older grove where the branches are above the head is best. One person is the pusher. The pusherman or woman selects a tree and stands with his or her hands on it at all times. The rest of the group are finders or spotters. Finders are blindfolded and are started about twenty yards from the pusher. Their task is to locate the pusher and tree. Spotters keep the finders from falling into holes and stepping onto nasty things. If the spotter is kind he or she can tell the finder when they have wandered too far off the target.

"Sharks and minnows" is like playing tag blindfolded. One person is blindfolded as the shark. The minnows have to slip by without being swatted. The game can be made more interesting by blindfolding both sharks and minnows, or just the minnows. Changing the terrain or lighting conditions, or using more physical techniques and weapons, can advance the learning.

"Land mines" is a blindfolded variation of "sharks and minnows" in which the exercise area is covered with "land mines." Focus mitts and Frisbees make excellent mines and don't shred the players. Blindfolded participants move from one end to the other of a "mined" area without touching or running into a mine.

Cues, Ruse, and Clues

Crossing hands the rooted person sinks.
Power is gained when an opponent enters your circle of life.
The immovable is created through moving into strife.
The circle is whole when inner and outer links.

Continuous attack is better than distraction.
A strong front gate is better opened from the side.
Attacking the attack will quickly lessen pride.
Maintaining a calm center is the strongest action.

The adept feels the opponent's intent before movement.
Eyes bright, tongue up, teeth tight, smile.
Soft breath, easy talk, relaxed, and hard to rile.
Avoiding intimidation is a way to contentment.

CHAPTER EIGHT

Teaching and Psi Abilities

To be both a speaker of words and a doer of deeds.
—Homer, sage and poet, *Iliad*, circa 700 B.C.E.

Nam et quit bene imperat, paruerit aliquando necesse est, et qui modeste paret, videtur, qui aliquando imperet, dignus esse. (The man who commands efficiently must have obeyed others in the past, and the man who obeys dutifully is worthy of being some day a commander.)

Marcus Tullius Cicero, senator,
De Legibus, circa 52 B.C.E.

Le monde recompense plus souvent les apparences des mérite que le mérite même. (The world often rewards the appearance of ability rather than the ability itself.)

François, Duc de La Rochefoucauld,
Réflexions, ou Sentences et maximes morales, 1665

Dojo Pedagogy

Responsibility, self-discipline, honesty, compassion, and calm are learned behaviors developed best by daily lessons. Character is cultivated both consciously and subconsciously in the little lessons we receive in the open observation of life around us. These lessons are reinforced by the actions of people around us until they become habits. Cowardice, deceit, treachery, greed, and wantonness are as natural as desirable human characteristics, and are learned in exactly the same manner. Creation of an environment where learning takes place is as much the responsibility of the teacher as is the content of the lessons. The media of presentation can be as important as the specifics of what is taught.

Dojo means "place of learning a discipline" or "way under a stick," implying that what is taught may be beaten into the student, or that the "way" is a physical as well as a mental art. The art of strategy *(heiho)* operates on two levels, the visible and invisible. The *kwoon* or *dojo* that emphasizes the invisible aspects of *budo* is thought of as a temple. Martial arts based primarily on the physical aspect of the techniques are usually sports, and can kindly be described by politically correct phrases such as, "The elevator doesn't go to the top floors," or, "The wheel is still spinning but the hamster is dead." When you use the temple ideal to evaluate a *dojo*, you'll find that most fall instead into the sweaty-gym category.

Whether the *dojo* is more a temple of learning than a gymnastic/aerobic parlor, with or without weapons, will be quickly seen in the conduct of the students. How do they act? Would you want your friends or children to act that way? Is naturalness or artificiality prized? Is there lots of bowing, scraping, and sucking up? Does the *sensei* require protection? How important is the hierarchy? What is the bill and how often is it presented?

Do the people studying there seem to be having fun? Do they regard their *sensei* with an awe that might be better reserved for a high-ranking military or religious figure, or with the respect and friendship with which we regard a superior teacher? Do there appear to be some major problems around inflated egos? Does the instructor, or do the students, use character-assassination techniques to keep students away from other instructors? ("Morris is a fraud, that stuff isn't part of real *ninpo,*" "Morris is a only a hobbyist, he doesn't get the real stuff.")

Do the teaching exercises reflect the reality of the times, or should a warning be posted indicating that individuals in the mirror are dumber than they appear? Most Americans have some street smarts and seldom leave an arm hanging out in the air unless there is some serious pain involved. Is there actual contact so students can learn what it is like to be hit, punched, and thrown about, as that is what happens in a real fight? One moment of shocking hands-on experience can be worth hours of kicking and punching air. Most people get started in the martial arts to do or avoid some serious ass-kicking. Teachers who forget that part of the discipline is to survive and conquer emphasize aesthetics over pragmatics to the detriment of what they teach. Often those who speak primarily of the beauty, discipline, and self-development inherent in the *dojo* haven't had to use their art on the street. Their pontifications should be assessed with caution. A taste for brutality reflects human reality.

Does the instructor use simulation and role-playing so the students can get a feel for different schools and attitudes of retreat and attack? Does the instructor have knowledge of various schools and their methods so the students can gain a familiarity with what he or she is likely to face, or is everything taught from the perspective of the particular school? A little knowledge can be a dangerous thing.

Is there a standardized curriculum so students have an idea of what he or she is supposed to know and do at a particular level of expertise? Can the curriculum be adapted for the student who is handicapped or athletically challenged? Are the senior students people you would want for neighbors or people who would offer friendship? A *ryu* often becomes an extended family. If you are a hobbyist, can the instructor handle your attitude that being a martial artist isn't the most important goal in your life? *Budo* is not even for everyone in *budo.*

And perhaps the most rigorous test: do the students perform at the same level or better than the teacher? A really excellent teacher conveys not only technical expertise but the attitudes and behaviors associated with the skillful and professional. A really excellent teacher conveys the feelings, excitement, discipline, and devotion with good-will and humor to the initiate, so they too will come to love the art and pass it on. (I have many students and friends whom I consider far superior to me in their areas of expertise.)

Are there older practitioners in the *dojo*, or is it primarily for kids? That alone should tell you to continue your search. (When the average human being lived about thirty years, Ponce de Leon's search for the fountain of youth made sense. In today's world there is no shortage of either youth or the aged. What might make a more valuable quest for the average martial art practitioner today is a fountain of smarts.) Studying the softer martial arts, such as *tai chi,* is associated with intelligence, health, and longevity.

If students or strangers insist on challenging you, simply turn up the heat. You can also develop a fighter or two that they have to go through before playing with you. When I had a relatively large *dojo,* I would occasionally have to entertain a smart-ass who wanted to take me on. Most fighters are too lazy intellectually to submit to disciplined training—unless you deliver them a serious whupping that gets their full attention through seeing their death or dismemberment. Furthermore, never, unless it is a ruse, become engaged with the challenging stranger's game. You have the choice of weapons. Choose your knights.

Spinal-Marrow Clearing

A teacher needs spine. If you find you are dealing with someone who is relatively spineless, here is a little exercise that helps eradicate that condition. Many of life's problems would disappear if only people would take a stand more quickly. This is a simple meditation that can help clear out any blockages in the spine and help keep (or make) the marrow within the spine healthy. I would definitely recommend it before doing kundalini meditations. It might be a good idea to combine this meditation with the healing screen and secret smile. This technique was road-tested by and on Wayne Oliver.

1. Loosen up your spine. This can be done by stretching, yoga, or *tai chi*. Be particularly attentive to the stretching and rotating of the neck. Let the head fall forward and stretch as it is easier on the nerves lessening the shear.

2. Hit the seated or standing position of choice. Relax and begin the deep belly breathing. Close your eyes. Actually *feel* the spine open up and relax.

3. Inhale and see that you are inhaling a pure white mist into your nose, down the functional channel to the *tantien*, down into the base of the spine, and up the spine, cleansing and purifying as it goes up. (Yes, this is a long breath, so do it S L O W L Y.)

4. Exhale and feel all the impurities leaving directly out of your spine. This will look like a smoggy gray mist.

5. Repeat steps 3 and 4 ten times or until the spine is adequately cleansed. These two steps are said to strengthen the spinal bones.

6. Become aware of a glowing silvery mist that floats in front of you. Inhale this white mist into your nose, draw it into your mouth, and swallow it. Exhale and bring it down to the perineum, or base of the spine.

7. Inhale and rotate this white ball clockwise. Exhale and rotate the ball counter-clockwise. Repeat this ten times.

8. Inhale and raise the purifying light into the spine, making it glow bright. Make sure to keep in mind that this energy is brightening and feeding the spinal marrow. Circle each vertebrae. As you exhale, do so directly from the spine. See all the nasty impurities leaving until only white light is exhaled. When you can embrace your own goodness, reverse the process.

Developing Psi Abilities

The following techniques were developed by Dr. John Porter, who teaches *bujinkan budo taijutsu* and *hoshinjutsu* in West Chester, Ohio. As soon as most people see anything out of the ordinary, they often dismiss it as nonsense or attribute it to demons, yet a great number of people in all walks of life believe in supernatural experiences. Supernatural experiences vary greatly in the frequency, intensity, and duration with which they happen to different people, and often change over time. They can occur at any time—awake or asleep, spontaneously or after long years of meditation, voluntary or involuntarily. These mental states may be due to an awakening of supernatural or psychic powers of perception latent in all of us. At the height of such an experience—often called a Psi experience—effects are produced that can be transcendent, the mind is divinely intoxicated.

Though often regarded as occult or New Age, many subtle phenomena have an empirical or scientific basis. Physicians are interested in how *chi* contributes to healing, and attempt through clinical observations to discover how they work. Many professionals who consider themselves scientists often associate visual hallucinations with schizophrenia or other mental disorders. This does not mean that nonpsychotic people do not have supernatural/visionary experiences. Many, in fact, do! A general term to include mystical and all paranormal experience of the mind, often used by Western scientists who study nonpsychotic "supernatural" phenomena, is "Psi." I refer to "Psi" and "Psi energy" to convey the idea of paranormal and psychic phenomena.

Several considerations apply when designing a Psi training program for yourself or for others. First, you need clear goals and objectives for the training sessions. When there is a perceived purpose of activity, the ability to learn is increased. Second, take time to develop the most basic and simple skills. Always progress from easy to more difficult. Most importantly, emphasize safety. Use a spotter. When learning difficult gymnastic techniques, coaches stand near the athlete to ease their fall, should something go wrong. In the same sense, practitioners of advanced Psi techniques should have a training partner or a friend to act as a kind of a spotter.

By the time I was in college I had experienced several different types of Psi. There was no doubt that I could receive stimulus from something other than the five senses. However, coming from a small town in the midwest United States, I had very little exposure to any concepts of the paranormal or Psi experiences. In graduate school a professor was writing a book on ghosts and other Psi phenomena that had been seen in northern Ohio. As his research assistant I traveled to as many of the site locations as possible. This was many years before there was any public interest. At about 95 percent of the locations there was no encounter with Psi energy.

After the book was published, another graduate student came to me and said he had experienced a Psi energy of extreme negativity on campus. He wanted me to check it out. I agreed, but to specific terms. We selected several dates so that I could choose the night and time of the inquiry. This was necessary to reduce the chance that there might be human manipulation. Also, I wanted to be able to bring an additional person as a witness to the event. This provided more security for me while I was in a meditative state. I was always more afraid of human intervention than encountering Psi energy.

Near the location of this evil energy was a long row of short, round, cement benches. They were about four feet in diameter and placed just a few inches apart. Behind the benches was a railing, and about a ten-foot drop to ground level. There were cedar trees close together growing from the ground level to about ten feet above the level of the benches on the terrace. They provided a relatively safe background from humans.

According to the information I had received, one of these benches was the source of the negative Psi energy. However, I was not told which one. I began to walk across the benches, feeling the Psi energy of each one. Soon I stepped on a bench and began to feel the negative Psi energy. I wanted to check out the next one to compare the energy level. As I stepped onto the next bench the feeling actually got stronger. After comparing the negative Psi energy level of several benches in that area, I was finally able to determine the bench central to the focus of negative Psi energy. It was so strong that it was radiating fifteen to twenty feet in all directions.

The Psi energy strategy for this encounter was for me to sit in the middle of the negative source of Psi energy and meditate. In this meditative state I was to contact and possibly communicate with the negative energy. The two people that were with me as observers sat next to a nearby building about fifty feet away, with their backs to the building wall, watching me.

As I went deep into my meditation I felt a small hole opening up underneath me. I was being pulled into the hole. It was like going down the hatch of a submarine. I could see the hatch door being closed. I tried to physically struggle to prevent the door from being closed and get back up to the surface, but the negative energy was too strong. I gave up physically. I knew that I had to use the positive Psi energy of the universe, which I think of as God. All of a sudden I was thrust back on the bench and heard the door to hell slam behind me.

Before the experience my colleagues and I had agreed not to talk to each other until we had written down what was experienced by each person. Both observers identified, independently, that I had disappeared for a short period of time. I believed in positive Psi energy much more after this experience, and I believed my positive Psi energy was increased. To a large degree, evil spirits generally avoid me. The downside to this ability is that it makes it very difficult to investigate simple negative Psi energy occurrences, as much of this energy is dispersed when I am in the area. During graduate school I met Dr. Morris. We have exchanged ideas as well as trained together on and off for nearly twenty years. The following exercises will be familiar to my students and many of his.

Meditation

A sound understanding and practice of meditation is fundamental in developing all types of Psi ability. Few martial arts classes pay any attention to meditation. Some schools try pseudo-meditation every now and then, just to be able to claim that they actually include meditation. Generally such meditative exercises are static, limited, and not adaptable to the changing and varied physical techniques being taught. Most martial arts, yoga, and other meditative classes confine themselves to using the lotus or *seizan* posture. There is a range of sitting, arm, hand, and finger postures. In a sense, the physical body parts can be specifically positioned, along with specifically selected breathing patterns, to enhance specific results. The meditation used in many classes is a form of Zen meditation, where the mind is emptied. In reality, this is a long-term meditative process, generally ineffective for most North Americans. In the West we want immediate results. Western people do not want to sit facing a cave wall for a dozen years to gain some enlightenment or Psi abilities.

There are different styles of meditation. Quiet, trancelike meditation is beneficial for some areas of development. Some enlightenment and Psi abilities can only be developed, though, through active and/or interactive meditations. The mental state used in active and interactive meditation unites personal Psi energy to the universal flow.

Begin with a meditation to improve your ability to focus a thought. As you begin to settle into a meditative state, pay attention to your breathing. Count your breaths as you breath out. Begin with one, then two, and so on until you reach the count of nine. When you reach the number nine, begin the count again starting with one. In the beginning, students will often get into to the teens before they realize that they went too far. Practice this elementary skill until you can do it consistently for five minutes.

Next, add a thought while inhaling. The first thought should be the word *focus*. At this level, breath in the thought-word *focus* then breath out in the counting pattern. Then substitute a thought-word for the word *focus*. This should be a word that has particular significance in your life that you would like more of, like *openness, clarity, calm, solidity,* or *letting go.*

One of the symbolic expressions of this meditation is that you are breathing in a part of the thought-word energy that exists in the universal energy around you. Counting keeps the mind focused on the thought-word. This is an excellent meditation technique for use in sleeping, healing, or walking meditation.

Create Energy

The creation of Psi energy emitted from the body is commonly generated from active and interactive meditation. A simple form of energy creation is to form a ball of energy between your hands. This ball of energy will become polarized and will have a magnetic field. With practice and breath control, the ball of Psi energy can be made larger or smaller. In extending this active meditation you can begin to toss the ball of Psi energy back and forth from one hand to the other. To continue to develop control of the Psi energy, throw it over an obstacle, bounce it off a wall, and then throw it to another person. Move perception around the room or area in the woods. Look for a secluded area in a woods if you choose to try this exercise outdoors. In an open park many people may feel self-conscious about nonparticipants who may be in the vicinity, and parks have many distractions to working with subtle energy. This is a fundamental skill to the Psi energy exercises discussed later.

Feeling Energy

One student will sit in a meditative posture feeling the aura around his or her body. Another student should stealthily walk around the first student and occasionally penetrate the aura but not physically touch the student. After the second student is finished and backs away, the first student can compare the Psi energy experienced to that which was actually given.

Building a Sanctuary

One of the initial personal meditations is to teach students to create a mental sanctuary. Time and care need to be considered in constructing this sanctuary. Therefore, it may take several meditations to complete. In fact, the first design may not be appropriate for future needs. From the sanctuary a person can train, find solace, or have secret areas to enter, such as the "room of ten thousand directions."

External Connections

Allow yourself to begin the process of connecting to the world, the cosmos, infinity, and the universal energy. Become sensitive to the subtle energies and movements that are around us all the time. Start with feeling the air around you. Learn to feel the Earth move. Becoming connected may actually cause you to lose balance. In the same manner, become sensitive to all your senses. Learn to hear clouds move on a quiet day.

The symbolic use of colors, sounds, and mantras enhances the Psi energy experience. The practitioner should choose one system, whatever it is, and stay with it. Changing color systems will distort the intended symbolism. Sound is different. In any language there are a variety of words that mean the same or similar thing as another. Therefore, being able to choose a sound from a variety of languages will not distort the symbolic essence of the meditation. The Psi intent of the sound is what is important. In developing Psi energy for martial artists, the meditation often must be in a more active or interactive form.

Meditative Travel or Astral Projection

Although Psi energy seems to travel instantly, it has certain limitations. That is, Psi energy has the potential to go anywhere in the universe instantaneously. This means that Psi energy travels much faster than the speed of light. The fact that Psi energy is infinitely curious significantly restricts its speed. It is not a simple matter of going from one place to another if your Psi energy has never been there before, especially if there are interesting things to see along the way. Psi energy wants to know every tree, crack, and blade of grass along the way. Once these details are known, the Psi energy can then quickly move past that area until it reaches the next unfamiliar area. The process then continues. Therefore, when using Psi energy to travel to a distant location or city, the initial meditations will only cover a portion of the distance. Meditative traveling to another city may take several attempts. Several meditations may be needed to reach a destination only fifty miles away. The good news is that once learned, always learned. Later, one route can be added to others to increase quick destinations.

In the same manner, you can travel across the cosmic universe or through time itself. You may even be able to find other Psi energy travelers to join with you on your journey. Meditative travel can become part of your daily routine. Late in the evening, just before you go to sleep, use Psi energy to walk the perimeter of your house. View your windows and doors for security. See if you left anything in the yard that should be taken care of. Go through your house, room by room, looking for potentially dangerous situations or lost items.

The first time I successfully consciously astrally projected was about twenty years ago. I began by using meditation, through which means I could perceive my awareness, leave my physical body, and float to the ceiling in the upstairs room I was in at the time. I was able to see and recall location of items in the room, including the furniture and small decorative items. After practicing moving about the room in the altered state of consciousness for a few minutes I wanted to explore my capabilities further. I decided to go through the ceiling. I was briefly in the crawl space, then decided to go up through the roof. At the time I was unaware of a wind storm that was going on outside. The wind caught my essence and began to blow me around uncontrollably. Fortunately, the wind blew me back into the peak of the roof where I was able to get out of the wind long enough to go back down into the house.

I decided to return to my physical body. However, another essence was trying to take over my physical body. Perhaps it too was blown into the house by the wind storm. I attempted to struggle with the essence but was unsuccessful. At some point I felt that the only way to be able to regain unity between my spiritual essence and physical body was to create a loud external noise. This might frighten the other spirit enough to allow me to slip back into my body.

I had the feeling that I had experienced this situation before, and that a loud noise had occurred, allowing me to successfully re-enter my physical body. At that moment there was a very loud clap of thunder and I was able to jolt into my body. My conscious instantly woke up. As I awakened I fell onto the floor, as if I had just freed myself from physically wrestling with someone.

The location of astral projection occurs just above the eyebrows, at the site of the third eye. Sounds will help you in the opening of the portal. Some chant the syllable sound, "hick." "Aum," chanted in a high pitch, will also open the portal.

Dream walking

Dream states are sometimes used like astral projection, but the feeling is different. In my state of dreaming there exist parallel worlds, or dimensions. For over a quarter of a century I have regularly dreamt about specific locations and people. The locations range from abstractions of this world geography, to locations that may seem similar to something in this world, and to locations that are totally of the other dimension, yet always consistent. During these dimension walks I experience changes in weather, including snow, sleet, rain, wind, and sunny days. There is day and night, evening and morning, and everything in color. There are people, or entities, that I recognize as inhabitants of that dimension. Often I will have discussions with some of them, telling them stories about what it is like to be in a physical human body.

Among the more subtle events I have found is that at times I get tired in this dimension. In this other dimension I will go to sleep and began to dream and enter the next dimension. I have also practiced and developed the ability to read in my dreams. It takes me so much effort to focus to read that it often exhausts me and I wake up forgetting most of what I have just read.

There are times when I need to travel from one city to another. I have learned my ways to several cities, including landmarks and other small towns in between. Sometimes there have been road closures or other causes to detour. I can see the route signs and will from time to time change to different routes.

In the small towns, I have become familiar with the stores and shops, especially on the main streets. I can give directions to other entities in this dimension and can anticipate alternate streets to use depending on the time of day or circumstances of perception.

Through introspective analysis (not through the use of an over-the-counter Freudian dream book) I have been able to understand some of what is going on in this dimensional state. Each individual physical building, store, or house represents a particular area of my life. Each specific location is consistent and congruent to a specific area of life. The interaction and relation of the people indicate what is happening in those areas. However, it is not always directly evident and often needs further scrutiny and decoding.

I work at being as aware as possible within my dream dimensions. Recently I have been working on finding the portals between dimensions. About a year ago I fell out of the dream dimension about five feet onto my bed. I was able to see the umbilical-like cord that connects the dimensions. Since then I have been trying to find the way back to this point from this side of reality.

Sparring and Gaming as Psi Tools

In many programs, sparring is the reward of personal expression after hours upon hours of rote mechanical training of physical techniques. Often the subtle concepts of Psi are overshadowed in sparring, giving way to an emphasis on speed and power. The reason for this is that many teachers are gifted athletes, whose physical qualities of speed and strength have been heightened from years of concentrated training. Statistically, very few participants win tournaments. In fact, the exact number is one winner per classification per tournament, regardless of the number of participants. Therefore, the limited emphasis on speed and power may actually have detrimental psychological effects on marginal participants.

Consider approaching training from the philosophical view that there will always be someone bigger, faster, stronger, with more weapons, and with different choices of location for attack. By developing Psi energy in sparring, participants can learn to move out of the path of an attack before the aggressor actually physically moves. This gives the illusion of improved reflexes.

100

The reality is that the defensive body movement is not caused by an analytic perception of physical movement by an aggressor; it is the response of a negative power intention to cause harm by the aggressor. This negative power emitted by the aggressor is perceived by the sixth sense of the defender.

A second important psychological aspect of sparring, or self-defense, is that the two individual Psi energies combine into one energy during the confrontation. In other words, instead of having two separate individuals sparring with each other, there is a single set of Psi energy dynamics that is comprised of two or more separate Psi energy sources. This psychological perspective is subtle. Yet, using Psi energy in sparring or self-defense is fundamental to the improvement of ability.

There are numerous exercises and variations of exercises that can be included in sparring to develop Psi energy. The exercises listed in this book will provide a well-rounded base of experiences for developing Psi energy in sparring. All of the exercises listed are done blindfolded. As in all exercises, safety should be stressed. In these exercises, the focused intention of physical harm by the attackers is essential. Without this quality the experience will have little value.

1. Kicks, punches, or weapons: The defender will be blindfolded and the attacker should be sighted. Work on angles of attack and levels of techniques familiar to the participants. The speed of the attack should be very slow! The purpose of this exercise is not to react to physical perception, but to mental intent of harm. Therefore, it is much more important that the attacker focus strong mental intent upon the part of the defender's body where the resulting attack will impact. In the same manner, the defender should not suddenly change the speed of the sequence to an all-out response. The defender should move at the same speed of the attack, maybe just a little faster. The second goal of the defender is to feel the exchange of body energy during the technique. The speed of an attack should not accelerate above half speed.

2. Grabs: Practicing grabs is similar to kicks and punches. The main difference is that the initial attack of grabbing does not cause injury to the defender. Therefore, the practice speed of this exercise can be increased to full speed. To extend these exercises, add multiple attackers.

3. Choose: This is a simple sighted version of defense against multiple attackers. Have the attackers decide who will attack first, second, and so on. Always begin with just two attackers. Increase the number of attackers as skill level allows. The attackers need to focus intent of harm, especially the first, or next attacker. The defender should initially position themselves in the approximate center of the attackers. The defender should then move into a position where they will be more at an advantage to defend from the order of attacks.

4. Greeting: Often in training class, a person extends his or her arm toward a defender to attack them in some way. In real life, people extend their arms toward us for a variety of reasons, such as to shake hands. Practice having a defender stand stationary. The attackers will walk toward the defender one at a time. The attackers will develop intent on extending their arm to the defender either as an attack or as a handshake. It is very important that the attacker does not try to deceive the defender in this exercise. The participants are learning the initial skill of reading intentions. To extend this exercise both the defender and the attackers may be moving toward each other, and/or there could be more than one potential attacker approaching from more than one direction. When using more than one potential attacker it should be predetermined among the attackers who will be aggressive and who will be friendly. Regardless of the number of potential attackers, only one should have the focused intent of attack. This is what the defender is trying to perceive. The final extension is to perceive the intent of everyone you shake hands with. Soon you will be able to determine whom you can trust and whom who you should be

cautious around. (It is often difficult for the attacker to quickly develop the intent of causing harm in a training session. This is because most participants are friends, or at least realize that their turn is next. Therefore, the level of harmful intent in training will always be very low compared to that of a real encounter. Becoming even a little sensitive to negative intent in training will often create the ability to easily sense danger in real combat situations. Daily life may not be as gentle.)

5. Tank: This game is as much fun to play as it is a multidevelopmental learning experience. It is especially useful with young people, or when some lighter training is in order. Tank requires more than one two-person team. Each team is composed of a commander who can see, and a blindfolded tank operator. The tank operator does all the work, include moving, shooting at the enemy, and finding new ammunition. The commander guides the tank operator by giving verbal directions only. The commander must relay direction, distance, aim, speed, and other essential information. When one tank operator hits another tank operator, the second tank operator's team is out. Use soft ammunition such as paper balls or bean bags. Limit the starting ammunition to two or three rounds. If the game is to continue, ammo must be salvaged.

6. Assassin: The assassin kills through a specific subtle look, perhaps the wink of an eye, or in passing an object to another. The method is agreed upon and known by all members of the group. The object is for the assassin to kill the members of the group before he or she is identified. Death is by poison so the assassin has time to move on before the victim collapses.

Image Projection

In our martial arts class, we work with image projection as a means of self-defense. This does not mean that we work on our personal image of looking good, but on projecting a kind of energy field that deters or allows the movement of others into specific areas. It is like a psychic obstacle course. The barriers created can be doors, walls, fences, moats, gates, or any variety of objects. They can be warm, friendly, and encouraging as well as cold and formidable. Through practice, the image projected by one person can be seen by another in exact detail. Often, in meditation, various aspects of one's persona can be seen—and it may surprise you to discover that what they project is not what they want to project.

Mental Barriers

Many people design their mental barriers in the form of a long high wall or an enclosed structure such as a castle. These mental barriers appear ominous and nearly impossible for anyone to get past. However, the use of an ethereal wind approach provides easy access to these earthlike barriers.

My mental barrier is a dark dense fog. I have no walls, gates, or guard dogs. As a matter of fact, most all physical objects within the terrain of my barrier are pleasant and easy to maneuver around. The problem is that the searching direction will be altered and the searcher will begin to get lost. Eventually the searcher will get tired of continually getting sidetracked or lost and will simply give up.

Shape-Shifting

When most people hear the concept of shape shifting they think of a human becoming an animal. This form of shape-shifting is generally of little use outside of a hunting-and-gathering society. (Shamanistic applications used by Dr. Morris tend to place an unnecessary burden of confidentiality on your friends.) A more practical version of shape-shifting is to be able to alter your perceived body size and weight. This will allow you to accomplish more, hide better, climb, fight, and attain what is needed if you can take control.

In this exercise, the perceived weight of a person can be experienced to be significantly altered by several people at the same time, within a matter of a few minutes. To begin, there must be at least five people. Six people is optimal. Have one person lay on the floor or the ground and begin to meditate. In the meditative state that person should focus on becoming as light as a feather. The other people kneel around the person meditating, two at the legs, two at the trunk of the body, and one by the head. After about five minutes of meditation, those around the meditator will simultaneously lift the body. The body will rise with relative ease. Then the meditator will focus on becoming as heavy as lead. After another five minutes or so the others will attempt to lift the same person. This time it will be very difficult, if not impossible, to lift the same person who just minutes ago was light as a feather.

Feng Shui

I have only recently experimented with the Psi energy of *feng shui*. After identifying two specific areas of need in my life, I began to use the principles of *feng shui* to improve some of my deficiencies. I have found that even subtle considerations have made a noticeable difference. The basic premise of *feng shui* is to align your environment to allow your energy to flow.

Psi Games

Most good instructors will present learning experiences in a variety of methods that include variances in level of difficulty, safety, and fun. Referring to common experiences, both in physical activities and as analogies in verbal explanations, will improve the skill of transferring information.

There are many games that adults from all over the world have played as children. Two games that are excellent in teaching a variety of Psi skills are hide and seek and tag. Nearly everyone has played these games to some degree. The social phenomena experienced in the West is that when we reach the age that our physical abilities, understanding of the game, and developed intuitive movements provide mastery of play, we are considered too old to continue to play such "childish" games. If these characteristics are continued into adulthood, it is generally considered to be deviant or at least bizarre behavior, especially when practiced by an individual within the context of regular society. Including variations of these and other games into the framework of an organized learning session in a controlled or semicontrolled environment will help produce amazing results in a safe manner.

Hide and Seek

In the basic version of this game one person closes his or her eyes and begins to count while the other participants hide. The counter then moves about trying to find the hiders before they can return to the counting spot.

To develop Psi abilities, some modifications can be added. First, in the *dojo*, the seeker can be blindfolded. To allow for all participants to have Psi experience, the hiders may also be blindfolded. Stealth-walking should be included as an essential element of this exercise. Participants may also seek personal items such as shoes. A park or woods allows for many extensions to this game.

Find

This game is played by two people in a group. The first person is blindfolded. The second person walks about twenty feet away and sits on the ground. The first person attempts to walk to the location of the second person using their Psi energy. This is a simple introductory version. The exercise can be extended by increasing the distance, doing it outside in a woods, and placing one or more obstacles between partners. The person who is sitting can also increase their stealthiness in getting to their location. If a person has a particular problem with stealth, or their shoes are just squeaky, they may go out, around, and come back into their spot.

Gates

This exercise can be accomplished in the *dojo* very effectively. A simple version is to put two objects such as bean bags or focus mitts on the floor about three feet apart. Have one person focus on the space between the obstacles, hot or cold. The second person slowly walks to the gate to determine if the area is hot or cold. The concepts of safe or dangerous, opened or closed, or positive and negative may also be used.

Once this individual version is mastered, set up a series of gates side by side. Have one person meditate on each gate. The student will walk to each gate and determine its quality. In an advanced version, a type of Psi energy maze can be created. For students who are very gifted, ask them to describe the barrier being created by the meditating student.

Adventures

The following is a list of the type of extraordinary experiences that nearly anyone can accomplish. These kinds of extraordinary experiences will not only increase your core Psi ability, but may require the Psi energy to accomplish. This list is meant to be a sample, and is not inclusive in itself. The experiences should be from an area that is extraordinary, not from a vocation or hobby. For example, if you are a carpenter by trade, building something from wood at home is probably not going to be extraordinary. Becoming a world-class athlete or swimming across one of the Great Lakes from the United States to Canada is extraordinary. Try some of these to see how they affect you.

1. Stay awake for seventy-two consecutive hours.
2. Walk fifty miles at one time.
3. Complete a full triathlon.
4. Win a championship.
5. Drive across the country without sleeping.
6. Swim to another country.
7. Kayak across one of the Great Lakes.
8. Parachute out of an airplane.
9. Take a hot-air balloon ride.
10. Run from one city to another.

11. Run your own marathon through all the neighborhoods of a large city.

12. Broaden your artistic skills in fine arts.

13. Build something useful.

14. Learn to face negative life experiences with a positive attitude.

15. Earn an academic degree.

16. Study a religion other than your own and then study your own.

17. Change a negative habit, or overcome detrimental obstacles.

18. Get something you write published.

19. Travel to foreign areas.

20. Teach a class on what you do well.

Disclaimer

Please do not try this stuff at home. Practice under the supervision of an experienced teacher or mentor who will keep safety considerations in mind. Each person has a specific capacity of skill, thought, and energy. To some extent, a person can develop and grow in capacity. Eventually, the human essence will be filled to capacity. Any further skills or developments gained in one area will result in a skill lost in another area. Further, there is a perception of balance in the universe. An individual can flow with negative universal energies as well as with positive universal energies. These forces exist in parallel, and are not separate. If a person takes a step forward, he or she is one step closer to the end and one step further from the start. Developing high levels of Psi energy in the body may overload some body systems, causing various ailments or dysfunctions of the body not otherwise anticipated. Psychic energy is no different from physical energy. Each may be transformed into the other.

CHAPTER NINE

Life Skills of Mastery

Ars prima regni est posse invidium pati. (The foremost art of kings is the power to endure hatred.)

Seneca (the Younger), politician,
Hercules Furens, circa 0050

But the actions of those who hold great power, and pass their lives in lofty status, are known to all men. Therefore, in the highest position there is least freedom of action. (Ita in maxima fortuna minima licentia est.)

Gaius Sallustius Crispus, soldier and historian,
The War with the Cataline, circa 40 B.C.E.

A politician is a man who understands government, and it takes a politician to run a government. A statesman is a politician that has been dead for ten or fifteen years.

Harry Truman, great American president,
statement, 1958

Searching for Grace

Man as a tripartite being (mind, body, and soul) is a formula both ancient and true. For someone to live well in the modern world, mind and body must be nourished. To experience transcendental states, all three must be engaged with attention to the spirit. Budo—the study of strategy, the art of winning, exploiting advantage, or *heiho* —translates as "method of the warrior" and has a deeper meaning as "method of truth." The same *kanji* when translated back into Chinese reads "peaceful."

Psychologist Mihaly Csiksentmihalyi finds that for most people, the experience of flow or transcendent mastery of a situation emerges when a person's body or mind is stretched to its limits in a voluntary effort to accomplish something worthwhile, until self-awareness vanishes, time is suspended, and spontaneous right action becomes natural to the person. Anyone who watches Hatsumi demonstrate a technique quickly realizes that he seldom repeats a technique but continually shows *henke* (variations) based on the movement of the *uke's* body. This is one way to keep one's flow from drying up, as the challenge to create is always present. Hatsumi-soke states strongly that he teaches this way to model the behavior for the *godan* and above.

Let us share some stories from the peaceful warriors, and I will comment in parentheses. Some of these came as letters, some as e-mail. I've tried to preserve the flavor of the sender but have occasionally corrected spelling or hidden the identity of the writer for professional reasons.

From Denver comes this tale from a student of *ninpo*:

> Some weeks ago Shidoshi was demonstrating techniques of escaping from multiple assailants armed with weapons. He asked another student and me, the strongest people in the class, to fully apply *hanbo* to his neck. I was in back choking and the other student was in front applying massive force to the back of Shidoshi's neck. As Shidoshi escaped (effortlessly, of course) and immobilized the other student, he placed his hand, fingers

110

extended, on my left chest, above the pectorals, and calmly asked, "Do you yield?" There was virtually no pressure, yet I desired to comply, even though there was apparently nothing stopping me from continuing. I hesitated, and he asked again, somewhat more forcefully, but still calmly, "Do you yield?"

At this time, I noticed a flash of red coming from the side of Shidoshi's head, and I yielded. For several weeks thereafter, I could feel the very slight pressure of his fingers on my chest. Last week I asked him about this sensation. His response was that it had to do with a number of things that had not been discussed relating to the mystical side of the art, and that he could not begin to explain in the time frame that we had. Eventually, if I kept playing, I would understand. I accept this for the time being and have a much renewed appreciation for *ninpo*. From my limited study, I don't believe that this is a location of a *dim mak* pressure point, yet I have no doubt that serious injury could have been incurred. (It's a secret sword technique. Dick Severance has a bag full of them.)

Iron body/shirt or golden bell *kung fu* are collections of breathing, meditation, and self-striking techniques used to make the body incredibly tough. When you practice the techniques your skin thickens and tightens, your body becomes much less sensitive to pain, and the bones get heavier and whiter. You can suffer years of being thrown around to achieve this kind of toughness, or you can do the iron shirt techniques and speed it up to a couple of months. The following story happened to me.

I was driving into Ann Arbor to do a stress-reduction seminar for a General Motors parts plant. I was driving my Ford Bronco II; there was sleet and ice. The woman ahead of me lost control in a downhill curve and was sliding sideways into my path. I could either hit her or step on the brakes to find out where I would then skid. Being a nice guy, I stepped on the brakes and went slamming into the road divide at about forty miles an hour. My safety belt snapped off at the ceiling and I broke off the steering wheel with my chest and bounced my face into the radio as my legs jackknifed up into the top of the well, banging my knees. I watched the hood fold and crumble as the engine collapsed toward me. My first thought as I whiplashed back into the seat was that it was really going to hurt when the engine and glass caught up with me. Time slowed down while I bounced around inside the cab, and the small truck filled up with a flash of yellow light. Everything went still. The windshield didn't break. The car was totaled, but I was safe. I kicked open the bent door and climbed out. An Air Force colonel stopped her car and put out some flares to slow traffic. The woman I braked to keep from hitting was long gone. I pushed the Bronco off the side of the road so that it was out of the line of traffic, and after leaving a note for the police, hitched a ride into Ann Arbor with the colonel so I could do the seminar.

I had two small bruises on my knees, one small bruise on my face where I hit the dashboard, and one small one on my chest where I broke off the steering wheel. I think the yellow light came out of my body. I don't know how golden bell works, but I do know it does work. I've never felt any urge to replicate this particular adventure. In a similar vein is the story of a guy called Motor, who's the son of my best friend. He was stopped in his small Toyota truck when a car plowed into him, sending the truck cartwheeling and then rolling down the road. Motor said when the ride started he just relaxed into it. He didn't get a bruise, though the truck was demolished. Motor didn't report any awareness of energy phenomena beyond relaxing rather than tightening when the truck began to fall apart. Motor has a master's in nuclear physics and is very smart, if not particularly visually sensitive. Here's another story (via e-mail) from a reader and surfer of the Net.

> Hello Dr. Morris. Thank you for the info. I now train under Jack Hoban on Mon. & Wed. and Don Houle (a *shodan* of Joe Maurantonio) on Sat. When i asked Mr. Hoban if he taught chi kung or any sort of meditation, he replied with a big NO. When i asked one of my seniors there, she told me i can meditate at

home if i wanted to. They kinda seem to want to avoid being asked any such questions. But the way Jack teaches taijutsu is excellent. Most of the techniques make me crack up. The opponent just runs into them. (Jack is one of the best. And being a ninja master is his hobby too. He isn't wasting his MBA. Both Jack and Kevin Millis have rock bands. Kevin Millis is a fine professional musician and has made a life with his guitar and the budo seminar circuit.)

I've had some very weird experiences meditating. I'm just now getting over the "fear" of letting more, brighter energy circulate. I also got to experience what a spider in heat feels like:-) that's been bugging me for a long time especially since i don't have a girlfriend, but today for some reason i felt a tension/vibrating in my throat, concentrated on it, saw "blue" and i cooled down. Weird.

I first meditated when i was six years old. One of my cousins gave me Stephen Hayes's book *Spirit of the Shadow Warrior* in 1981. I'm twenty-one now. I actually tried the meditations at the end of the book, and i can remember feeling intense pain in my forehead every time i hit the position. Several years later in high school i got into zen & yoga and i was trying chi kung orbits from studying shaolin five animals. The problem was every time things got weird, i turned chicken and stopped. Shaking, colors, etc. One time in my junior year i felt energy rush up my spine from my genitals and it scared the living crap out of me, i stopped it when it reached the heart region and got up and took a walk. I didn't meditate again for a couple of months.

Bujinkan budo taijutsu has had a weird effect on me psychologically. For example, i don't mind being off balance or falling anymore, as i know i will just roll back up again. For some reason i can just "do" whatever i feel like without any anxiety or regrets anymore. As such, i figure its time to start sustaining the effects of meditation.

It seems i've been attracted to ninpo ever since i was very young. I'll leave out a lot of weird stuff, since i don't want to bore you, but for a while there i kept dreaming of Hatsumi-Soke. I guess it had to be my imagination right? After i studied your books, i finally decided to join bujinkan.

Lately, i've just been doing zen sorta. I just empty my mind and stuff just happens on its own, for example the throat chakra/blue thing. I guess that happened because of the tai-jutsu. When i first started, after rolls i had trouble breathing and a very exquisite feeling or sensation in the upper chest/throat area. It stopped after a while. I sometimes get a really icy-hot feeling in my stomach that spreads to the small of my back. I really should do the orbit/etc. but for some reason it seems i'm making faster progress just shooting for mushin. Every time i try to make the dan tien heat up, it won't. Every time i just sit and keep empty, it lights up. I don't know. (Follow your heart.)

As long as you're reading this, let me tell you about the first time i went to Jack Hoban's dojo. I came in about forty-five min-utes late, sat there for a while watching the class, and since there was an uneven number of people, i figure that extra person could throw me around instead of waiting around for his turn. So i went up to Jack and said something like "Hello Sir. Since you have an odd number of people can i join in? I probably can't do any of the techniques, but i can just attack and get thrown around."

He seemed surprised for some reason, but said OK. He kept staring at me really weird, his eyelids were open all the way, eyes relaxed and not blinking. Anyway i was flopping around trying to do the techniques, and having the techniques done on me. After i screwed up a roll and was sprawled, my training part-ner just "accidentally" hit me in the head lightly with his hanbo.

He looked REALLY surprised. All of a sudden in a really fluid motion i got up, "disarmed" him, and was about to retaliate, when i caught myself and just presented the hanbo back in both hands to him. We both looked over at Jack and he just sat there staring at us with a strange look on his face. After that he just grinned as if he was amused every time he looked in our direction.

On Sunday i trained with David Greenberg. He is one of Doron Navon's students. I asked him if he read your books (he hadn't) but he said he remembers you from the 93 tai kai and says hi. I'm training with him next Sunday also. After that he's going back to Israel. He's a very good teacher. We even meditated(!) . . for . . . a whole . . . minute. Oh well :-).

Well, i hope the above didn't bore you too much, but i just figured i'd write you a short well . . . ok long . . . thank you for writing those books and the info you e-mailed me on how to find Jack Hoban and Joe Maurantonio! You've really helped me a lot. If you ever do a seminar or anything on the east coast be sure to let me know. I'll try to get those tapes as soon as possible. Thanks again. Chuck

Another story about a teacher I know too well:

Hi, Glenn! My name is Brian Jones. After reading your first book, I looked up Greg Kowalski and have been studying with him since January of '96. It's the best thing I've ever done. In the short time that I've known him, he has shown me how to "unlock" my real self and how to start peeling away the layers I've wrapped around myself for so long. Nobody else has been able to do this. The experience is kind of like shucking corn.

About three months or so into my training with Greg, I did a Rubenfeld Synergy session with him (Greg has trained for years with Ilanna Rubenfeld and is certified in her system of healing/therapy). We planned on going for a hike afterward. During the session my eyes were closed, and while Greg was working on my body I saw a very particular landscape with pine trees and rolling hills. I was viewing it from up high at the edge of a cliff. When I described this to Greg, he said something nonchalant like, "Gee, that's nice," and continued with the synergy session without further reference to my "vision."

After the session, we went on a hike at Sleeping Giant Park in Hamden, CT. We stopped at a spot that Greg described as his favorite place to relax/contemplate/get away from it all. As

I grabbed a sandwich to eat I looked out over the landscape. Greg said casually, "Look over to your right."

"Holy Shit!" Judging by the knowing smile that played across Greg's face, I know my face registered complete shock and disbelief at what I saw! It was EXACTLY the picture I had in my head during the Synergy Session! Keep in mind, I was new to all this and kept kind of quiet about it, for fear that what happened was not as it seemed. I've not really shared this with anyone, and still didn't feel comfortable at the time telling Greg how profound it was for me. It wasn't discussed again. I guess the baggage of my skepticism was at war with what I now know really happened.

Quite amazing . . . Glenn, I owe you a huge debt of gratitude for introducing me, via *Path Notes* to Greg Kowalski. Merely saying thank you is not enough. I hope that relating to you my experience in some way goes toward fulfilling that debt. (A little publicity won't hurt Greg. And I thank you for the story that illustrates how telepathy is more visual than most suspect.)

Matt Holcomb studies *bujinkan budo taijutsu* under Dr. Mike Fenster-shidoshi, judo and *sombo* under Grandmaster George Nobles, *hapkido,* and is one of my personal *chi kung* students. He is a competent *dan* in a number of nasty arts. Here is his story.

You going to Tai Kai? The financial end of it didn't work for me this year (me either). Although, as the Miss Congeniality prize, George Nobles (another member of the World Head of Family and Sokeship Council) has now adopted me as a judo student, so that's cool. He's putting on a seminar in sombo (PC for sambo) groundwork, and will probably do it down here for us, sponsored by the judo group. His wife is becoming a marital arts widow, and Patrick the six-year-old wild man has taken up judo. It's cool. Here's a funny story resulting from it which I sent to Nobles when he asked about a side comment I made. You might get a chuckle out of it too:

A fine Wednesday evening, I'm standing in the shower,

minding my own business and trying to relax after a taxing day. Suddenly, the shower curtain flies open, and my wife is standing there with a severe look on her face, and says, "We have to talk, your son just threw me!"

The story, as it was then relayed to me, is as follows. My son, all of six years old, has for a couple of years now occasionally accompanied me to my martial arts classes, a hobby of mine that borders on addiction in some people's eyes. It had been about eleven years since I had done any judo, I've been pursuing other arts of late, but the judo instructor at the dojo I train at was leaving. Given the fact that I had, at one time, done a fair amount of judo, I was asked about the possibility of taking over the group.

I had taken my son with me, as I normally do when it's not a late-evening practice, and we got to the dojo a bit early. As I was warming up, I asked him if he would want to learn anything. Up to this point, the answer had always been "No, I just want to watch," but I kept asking because I figured there would be a time when he'd be ready. This day, however, he said yes, so I taught him the first throw in the gokyo, de ashi harai, with some necessary modification due to the 180 pound and height differential between the two of us. Despite the size, he did quite well. I also showed him the typical kesa gatame, and within a few minutes he was throwing me down and jumping on me with some vigor.

When people showed up for the actual class, he appeared to lose interest, so he went back to watching. I conducted the class and we went home. Apparently, I didn't understand how important it was to him. The whole week after that session (session was on Sunday) through Wednesday he was bugging his mother to let him show her how he learned to throw.

Well, the fated day, with me in the shower, she finally gave in and said, "Look, I'll let you show me the throw, but I won't actually let you throw me." My son, not lacking in confidence after taking on Daddy, who is about twice Mommy's size, says they should move to the carpeted area off the hardwood floors.

Mommy says "Look, you don't understand, I'm not actually going to let you throw me. I'm just going to let you show me how you do the throw." Somehow, even after being married to a marital arts addict for over ten years, she missed the part about a properly executed throw working well despite large size differentials.

So, the six-year-old overgrown puppy launches off on Mommy with all his might. I do wish I would have seen it, to tell you the truth, for the way I heard it told she had a shocked look on her face all the way down. Then, to add insult to injury, he jumped on her and pinned her in fine form.

As the smoke cleared and I sat there in the bathrobe talking over the obligatory proper-use-of-marital-arts and Mommy-is-not-a-valid-target issues with my son, I leaned over and whispered to him, "Was it fun?" He broke out in a big smile and whispered back "Yes," and kind of giggled a bit. He then leaned over and whispered to me, "It was really easy, Daddy."

The next week, he was taking on the senior brown belt in the group, working on two new throws. I figured he'd do pretty well; he was only giving up about 130 pounds this time, and he's been reminded that Mommy is off the target list.

But, that fun stuff aside, I've been doing some interesting things energy wise I thought I'd pass on. Do a standard foot sweep mirror drill, stepping forward/back. When the person is just about to step forward, shoot a picture of the foot stuck to the floor/ground. (What you stick it with is up to you.) The effects I've seen range from slowing down to an outright stumble. Matt

Alan Brooks is an Australian engineer, vegetarian, yoga, massage therapist, and *hoshintao chi kung* practitioner and instructor. I usually stay at his house when I'm in Sydney, because he lives off Manly Beach and I like the view, food, conversation, and winter swimming. His thank-you letter reads:

> It was great having you stay with me, Glenn. I learned a lot and enjoyed every minute of it. Its a pity that you couldn't stay

longer. I would have liked to do a lot more meditation with you. You know when you went, all of your animal spirits, insects, strange apparitions, and the grotesque sort of faces I used to see when you were teaching me went with you. I'm back to my colors and fairy lights again, rather unexciting, but still mind-expanding and uplifting. I still feel the spiraling motion of energy, and now and then a splash of white as if a camera bulb went off in my third eye.

Its funny, but just like you said the day you left, the sunny weather turned to torrential rain and the ocean temp is now fifteen degrees. A bit chilly but good for raising the heartbeat and voice pitch. The tapes are great. It will take me a few listens to get it all. A couple aren't too clear as the background music drowns out your voice. (Everybody has some critic in them somewhere.)

Geoff Smith, Rose Smith, and Jean-Paul (JP) Vernon are *hoshin* students in Sydney, Australia. Rose and I became friends through correspondence after she read my *Path Notes,* through which she learned to heal herself of a death-threatening disease through *chi kung* and the secret smile. She later invited me down under to open a school, which seemed to ignite a bunch of political hotheads in what passes for *ninpo* in kangaroo country. Not wanting to miss a chance to visit one of the more beautiful places in the world, I accepted the invitation and had a great time training with fans, *karate,* and *jujutsu* players. No "real" *ninja* participated. I found Rose's fiancé to be grossly under-ranked and have corrected that with *bujinden* as well as enhanced his vocation by making him head of school for *hoshin* in Sydney. I asked these good folk from Oz to describe their experience.

Dear Glenn,

Now that the wedding is over, hoshin is IN with a vengeance, and the boys are now seriously considering the stakes in the first grading. We have recruited a new girl, and we hope for more members at our next BBQ. JP, G, and I have written this piece, and you might like to know that Leon (now second in the world at shotokan kata) sends the message that its "ditto for him" with all that is written.

Rose says,

I first had the idea of inviting Dr. Morris to come to Australia toward the end of '95. It was after reading *Path Notes* and trying some of his interesting theories. I really wanted to meet Glenn and ask him about the theories personally. I tried contacting him through his publishing company and was totally amazed when I received a reply! After a long series of obstacles and setbacks, we finally collected Glenn from Sydney airport in June 1997. Dr. Morris displayed his amazing escape techniques immediately by walking past FOUR of us at the arrival gate, and getting onto a bus to another terminal. That was the start of one big adventure for all of us connected with the traveling nuthouse affectionately known as "Dr. Death's Hoshin Tour Down Under."

One of the first things I noticed about Glenn is his uncanny ability to see what's going on through the back of his head. He has an amazing sense of energy about him, and I noticed that when he trained with "the girls" (i.e; Moi) that I was never left with a bruise, no matter how much the technique hurt. Bruises are the one thing I have come to expect when training with my husband and his friends, so I was pretty surprised at the way Glenn would put his hand over the affected area and voila! No bruise! Glenn also has a pretty freaky way of telegraphing energy to people, and we would actually rock when Glenn deliberately sent "the power" our way. One might say he literally "glows in the dark."

On the first evening of Glenn's visit, we were sitting around in Alan's flat chatting and asking questions. Alan's walls are a dark cream color, and provide a perfect backdrop for aura gazing. All of us were aware of a really bright corona around Glenn's head in particular, but the more observant noted bright blue in the outer ring. Glenn also had what appeared to be "wings" coming out from his heart chakra, green for love. Glenn actually left his auric image burned into our eyes (a bit like when you look at a light bulb) for some time after looking at him. I find this only happens when I have been looking at people with extremely high spiritual energy. One of the other things worth noting is the "activity" around Glenn. Several of the people attending workshops saw "otherworldly" critters around him, and one evening I was most definitely visited by his little Goddess friend. . . . I woke up with a fractured toe. . . . Figure that one if you can! Glenn is constantly attended by several of his "guides." Something else noted by the hoshin crowd out here. A few skeptics were definitely convinced after Glenn's stay, let me tell you.

I cannot speak about martial arts with any authority, since I am not a martial artist by any stretch of the imagination, but I must say that Glenn's hoshin techniques were not only highly effective, but extremely easy to learn. Glenn has really worked out a great system for women to learn self-defense in a very effective, safe way that doesn't keep you on the same boring technique for twelve years before moving to the next one.

Finally I'd like to point out that Dr. Morris is truly champion when it comes to personality (I'll have the check now, Glenn). We didn't know what we were getting with Dr. Morris. He could have insisted on staying in the best hotels, and getting paid top $$$ for every last thing. Instead he opted to stay in our houses, eat with us, drive with us, and generally be with us. He put up with our Aussie humor (Most Yanks never get it!) and was a really good sport in all areas. . . . Especially when he nearly slid into the fire pit during our fire walk. . . . (the edges were muddy). I'd also like to point out that all that stuff he says about only taking four breaths a minute is absolutely true. We put him in the water at Manly beach (June is our winter) and watched.

Jean-Paul says,

A certain wry charm exudes from the man known as Dr. Death; however, don't let that fool you into a false sense of security.

When you sit back and take a look at him, I mean a good look, Glenn has a pervading electric aura, and you certainly know he is there.

Most training was conducted outdoors, adding the enjoyment of fresh air, native flora and fauna (the birds!) to delight the senses, and of course great surfaces to be thrown, pummeled, kicked, jabbed and shocked on. Glenn has a fantastic training method: grab the closest person to use as a uke and apply pain accordingly. Well, after going through many bouts of pain (and one attempted come-on) I certainly had a great appreciation for his skill, ethic, generosity, sincerity, and his "touch of death." I found his techniques simple and effective. They provided a great way to remove yourself from trouble, oftentimes without even inflicting a cut or bruise, particularly hand-and-limb controls (let us bow down and "come to Jesus"). The training made sure you remembered the right technique for the situation. All this provided in the great outdoors and bushland settings of Australia, as well as visitations by a few Aboriginal/Australian spooks.

You may think that the Doctor has no sense of humor. Oh, contraire! This man knows how to party: fine wine, fine food, great people, and wrap it all up with stories and jokes. He certainly knows how to express his inner child. Glenn even went to the extent of stealing food from my dinner plate. No wonder everyone was laughing. Thanks for sharing, caring, and bearing ones' self with us, O Great One. Well, that's enough from me, now it's on to the Head of Spooks for Australia.

The Spiritual Head of Australia says,

Thanks for the title, Glenn. I'll never live that one down. When Rose first told me that I was to be the recipient of your teaching in PERSON, I thought that she'd flipped. However I soon discovered it was true and this is what I experienced.

I perceived an increase in energy when Glenn was around. Rather than see, I would experience a person's state of mind, glimpses of their awareness, so to speak. Too close when it came to tai jutsu. Watch out for Glenn's ura gyaku pin to the ground with optional wet willie! That was an experience in itself. Our talks on energy, guides, and spirits brought some interesting visitors and interesting situations.

One of the things that Glenn is really BIG on is the inner smile. I regard the inner smile as an effective tool for letting go of past negative experiences and creating a new, more productive self-image. I tend to be creative and travel to my future self, a (hopefully) much wiser and experienced me, where I can gain insight and much healing with a different perspective. It is good to allow your mind many viewpoints from which to draw. Mental pushups give you a more objective way of looking at life. It is imperative that you train your mind/spirit well, no matter what religion, belief, or background you are. One of the things that really impresses me about Glenn is the way that he has integrated a lot of mind work (brain food) into hoshin. Rest assured your body will want to become compost one of these days and what's left is what you are, your essence. I hope you have made it a good home.

The best martial artists are integrated with themselves and the world around them because they are at peace with themselves and the world. Having let go of anger and ego, they appreciate life. They are living a progressively enlightening "warriors way." A lot of today's martial artists could learn from Dr. Morris, a man definitely devoid of ego, and so humble that he stayed in our houses and sat on the floor to tell stories to us.

The taijutsu Glenn displayed was efficient and realistic. It also conveyed his personality, as your body is a vehicle for your spirit to express itself through. Good taijutsu helps, but your mind is most important. A Ferrari is great to have, but you have to know how to drive it. Glenn's chi was too good. . . . Ouch! It added the crucial edge to his techniques. I want to finish by saying that Dr. Morris is one of the nicest, most humble martial artists I have ever met. I really enjoyed our time together, and we are all waiting for his return.

Glenn, I've got the juicer ready for you, and Alan has been tuning up the birdseed porridge (wunnerful, wunnerful). Currently we number twenty-five members in Sydney, and we look forward to new blood joining the team and being shed. Cheers Glenn for the morale boost and for the sick, sick e-mails!

—The dashing lads and sheilas from down under. (I just seem humble and devoid of ego in comparison to the average Australian.)

Todd Smith, a great *nidan*, runs the Hillsdale College Arboretum *hoshin dojo* now that Tom Van Auken, a *godan* in *hoshin*, *sandan in isshinryu*, and *shodan* in *budo taijutsu*, is concentrating on *ninpo*, *karate*, and his own business in Jackson. Here's his e-mail:

i have really been having some freaky meditations when i meditate with my sword. i feel as if i am leaving my body, turning into the fog, and making my way through the woods around my home. this feeling is unexplainable. i think that it ranks right up there with sex. who knows maybe i just haven't been doing the sex thing right. have a good one!" (Get the Big Red Book, Todd! It is time. Todd found another really old sword that is as strange in its way as Lydia is in hers.)

Battlekat is a very clever executive that trained with me in New York and Florida. Since I couldn't make the *taikai* because of a science conference on our patented media for a bacterium that could be the cause of CFIDS and MS, I asked her to "sniff" about for me and check out an individual I was thinking about grooming for a knuckle and skull bout for some big money. She regards her ESP (Psi) skills as a form of scent. Here's her first report.

o-genki desu ka, sensei styx

jay was, well, interesting. i don't know him very well so i don't have a solid baseline to draw from, but from the way he smells and from the way others deal with him, i take it he can be extremely temperamental and a bit testy at a times. funny, because he was so nice to me that his unusual behavior was cause for comment, stared a lot too, when he thought i wasn't looking, and sometimes when i was. evidently, he also thinks that i'm sexy. i heard it in his head, plus he told me. my theory is that he developed a crush of some sort, perhaps as a result of the good vibes in the joint and the overabundance of free-radical testosterone blanketing the area. i'd also bet that he's used to women falling at his feet whenever he shows the slightest bit of interest. while I certainly enjoy beauty (and he is rather beautiful), i haven't fallen at anyone's feet in quite some time, which may have some sort of appeal. he seemed to enjoy it whenever i said "get away from me, jay" go figure. he's fun.

the boss tapped me from across the room at the reception the first time . . . it was very bright and similar to when taffesse helped me "clean my glasses" in the beginning before i rewired. it was very gentle and felt like a question/welcome. i sent back a bow/smile/thank you. the second time was when he came up to me and we were introduced by gina . . . he held onto my hand after shaking it and for a moment all my everything stopped in a very pleasant way. i have been feeling rather different ever since. i'm still discovering the things that have changed, one of which is my body, which seems to be streamlining all on it's own. the spelling thing seems to be leveling off. (She went through a period of spelling-skill loss.)

there were some interesting people outside of your group . . . one older guy who's face is very craggy and pleasant like a dried apple and wears a very old leather walk-about hat. i'm horrible with names. (Ed Martin-shidoshi, 10th dan, father of the twins.) He mind-sent a nice hello, and asked me verbally to come to a seminar that he's giving soon. i got quite a few seminar invitations like this minus the silent messages, and I got stared at a lot. there also seemed to be several guys better nameless who seemed to find some reason or another to be around me or to talk to me about not-really-anything. there was so much swirling in the air. i've never been around that much directed-head-noise that i started to feel like a bloodhound at a perfume counter. i did notice one or two people who were distinctly not happy about me being there, though they smiled very prettily at me, and i put on my best little-girl-lost-happy-to-meet-you-too-big-strong-man face, which at least kept me from being too much of a target. testosterone can be poisonous.

I also asked Battlekat to submit an anecdote concerning our relationship.

so we're talking on the phone, right? normal conversation, then, as we keep talking, things start to get light/bright around the edges of my vision like it does whenever i'm doing energy stuff. it's a feeling i've come to associate with a transfer of energy. i've gotten relatively used to the feeling, and i'm also kinda used to picking up vision/scent information from the environment of someone i'm talking to, especially when they are an "on" sort of person, so i'm not completely surprised when i start "seeing" something that looks like the blade of a circular saw (sort of looks like the negative of a black-and-white photo superimposed on my normal vision). when i asked you what it was, you told me that it was the outline of a Zulu herding god's mask that hangs on the wall of your office. (Bahule protects the cattle from illness, wild animals, and evil spirits.) cool!

so we keep talking, and things are progressively getting stranger and stranger in an unfamiliar way . . . i don't say anything about it, but i'm feeling more and more like i'm "not all there." my circuit-breakers are tripping like crazy (which has only happened in the past when there's a BIG influx of energy) and i'm jittery in a peel-me-off-the-ceiling kind of way. the feeling keeps getting stronger, and i'm way too amped at this point to focus enough to figure it out, so i just flow with it.

anyway, we get off the phone, and the sensation doesn't diminish at all. I feel like i'm about to fly away or something, and i'm pacing back and forth in my apartment like a caged animal. in a weird sort of attempt to ground myself, i go to the mirror in my living area to see if i look as crazy as I feel . . . boy, was i shocked! my face was half gone. there was just space in the place where the right side of my face should have been—i could see the normal living-room stuff reflected in the background through the space. the other half of my face looked like a biological rendition of a picasso painting, and my right arm and leg kept fading in and out. so of course I ran like the devil to the bathroom to see if a closer inspection would be any different, but it was exactly the same, even when my nose was an inch away from the bathroom mirror. now i'm excited as hell and ready to do some experiments with this "new me." i am nothing if not insatiably curious, but alas, the feeling starts to fade, and then my face came back. damn. it was fun while it lasted. i remain . . . very small kat :-)

CHAPTER TEN

Magic and Mysticism: Experiences from the Field

On ne choisit pas pour le gouverner un vaisseau celui des voyageurs qui est de la meilleure maison. (The captain of the ship is not chosen from among the passengers coming from the best family.)

Blaise Pascal, thinker, *Pensées,* 1670

Mann muss etwas sein, um etwas zu machen. (One must be something, in order to make something.)

Johann Wolfgang von Goethe, writer/poet,
in conversation, 1828

Be ashamed to die until you have won some victory for humanity.

Horace Mann, educator,
Commencement address at Antioch College, 1859

History Lesson (That You Will Not Be Doomed to Repeat It)

Deep in the bowels of the Lascaux Caves in France we find the paintings of the Bird Man, dating back twenty thousand years. He lies in trance state, wearing his bird mask, arms flung out. His staff is topped with spread wings at his side, and a bloody buffalo is visualized before him. Seven thousand years later in a nearby cave we find another painted figure draped in animal skins, tailed like a wolf, wearing the head and antlers of a stag, dancing at the edge of a herd. These were not ordinary hunters of the late Paleolithic, but more likely shaman using animal spirits to fetch the game through sorcery. Throughout the world, similar figures appear scratched and painted onto rocks and carved in temples as tributes to those who worked the magic. These precursors of modern scientists and religious priests practiced a daunting natural philosophy that parallels science and phenomenology in organization if not content. These ancient shaman laid the ground work for sorcery, alchemy, magic, science, and religion.

Magic, through the use of spells, and religion, through the use of prayer, share the idea that one can train and concentrate the power of thought. Thought can cause effects outside of the thinker's body. Thus, thought properly cultivated through intent can make changes in the world. The religious suppose the gods hear your plea and make the changes for you. This is called answered prayer. The shaman and sorcerer suppose these changes are caused through the willpower of the individual alone. This is called casting. The truth may lie somewhere between as there are dwellers in the gap.

At any rate, mankind has dabbled with the abilities and disciplines necessary to shift reality for a very, very, very long time. The literature of magic assures us that the gifts or talents are rare, and require iron discipline as well as rocklike faith, which are not particularly attractive in an age of fast food and quick delivery. The steep climb and rarefied company do attract some members of the *budo buyu*. The climb from innocence into darkness and back has parallels in the painstaking pursuit of knowledge that attracts the true martial artist. And, of course, one must risk hell to achieve heaven so your strategy should preserve the integrity of your soul.

As magick is reviving a popular interest in alchemy and other fun arcane disciplines, the occult student is forced to separate the wheat from the chaff to find real sustenance. Just as magic was displaced by the easier and more predictable scientific method to become a realm of charlatans and credulous for the most part, so fared organized religion. The modern age need not accept the rejections of the past without examination. The neuropsychological method of anthropology is growing in acceptance since I first mentioned it in *Path Notes,* though some still refer to them as "shamaniacs." The method does provide a better explanation of these cave wall drawings than the "this is how they taught hunting, and we aren't sure what these swirls over here mean" school of scholarly divination. Some of the wall painting representations appear quite familiar to the modern alchemist, if not to the modern anthropologist.

Carl Jung, the great Swiss mystical psychologist, spent many years immersed in the study of alchemy and meditation. He was trapped by paralysis of analysis. His study did not complete the doing, but he observed that the standard religions of his day "were not the last answer to the manifold enigmas of man and his soul." Spirits spoke to Jung and he recorded their visits, but he was not polite enough to return the favor. He did not understand *giri.*

Richly symbolic and somewhat secretive with good reason, the intricate counter-culture of Western alchemy flourished between the fourteenth and eighteenth centuries, producing a great body of art and literature stressing reverence, work, meditation, and the need for prayer, as well as secrecy and suffering. The union between male and female, sun and moon, yang and yin, *yo* and *in* is fundamental to all alchemical works West and East dealing with the rebirth of the soul. In Western alchemy energy aspects are often discussed or portrayed through concrete examples such as paintings or statues of androgynous figures having both male and female characteristics—one side bearded and armored, the other clean-shaven and gowned. Process descriptions such as "the first coniunctio is followed by the nigredo," a stage of black putrefaction often compared to crippling depression. "The fourth coupling, called losis or red, precedes the recovery of the elixir of life surrounding the prima materia." Losis is symbolized by a sexy broad-hipped peasant girl with unbound hair balancing a jug of water decorated with the face of a lion on her head. Losis stands bare-footed on a large ball in which a burning triangle, point up, is carved. What could be clearer than that?

Sometimes sexual energies were represented by double dragons with their necks entwined. Anyway, the *ecclesias* (state-supported churches) did a good job of stamping out the public practice of alchemy by the end of the nineteenth century. What the churches missed hidden deep in the caves, the scientific method traditionalists will continue to attack.

Tibetan Buddhism has preserved the *dharma* (teachings and commentaries of the Buddha) in the East. I find that the karmic viewpoint coincides with some of my odder experiences. The commentaries on meditation, recently shared and translated for Westerners, have the following commonalties.

The basic space of emptiness (void) and wisdom are integral. They cannot be separated into a duality without artifice. *Prana* and mind are merged with the spontaneous appearance of a *dakini*. Tantra is divided into Father Tantra (yang) and Mother Tantra (yin), and nondual tantra *(kalachakra)* is often perceived as bliss. This achievement of integrated aspect is understood as the totality of Buddhahood, referred to as *Sambhogakaya*. This is a process that states that effect is not a result of effort but of approach. *Shamatha* and *vipashyana* are the primary tools and should be practiced together. *Shamatha* consists of nine levels of meditative practice directed toward settling the mind in calmness or equanimity. *Vipashyana* is usually practiced after *shamatha* is completed or is a natural result of the practices, and is concerned with knowing phenomena through examination and analysis. The results of *shamatha* are the *siddhi* (magicks), and the result of *vipashyana* is liberation from the wheel of *dharma*. (Yippee.)

Tales from the Great Web

When she was fourteen, Lisa smoked a lot of marijuana; she was also learning to meditate, and the combination of the two states of altered consciousness took her into kundalini arousal. For four years she burned in the orgasmic ecstatic light of one who actually lives and feels God's presence. She was a smart and pretty girl when she went off like a bottle rocket into the void. She had a charisma that drew people to her like a flame, and she could at least witness to her vision if not explain it. At eighteen the drug-induced startup ran out of endocrine fuel, and she crashed into the dark and material reality of separation from the light. It was the darkness described by St. John of the Cross, the black night of the soul cut off from the nature of love, the deadening nigredo of the alchemists. Suddenly her persona was fragmented and feelings were vague, out of touch. Her reality was gray, full of pain from a fried nervous system and dried endocrine system, oddly functioning immune system, and terrible, unexplainable lack of color and appropriate feeling.

She howled with rage and pain at this new predicament, wept from longing, and hungered for her former self. Her nervous system no longer functioned properly. She was a victim of EMF overload. She had missed a lot of education during the four years of continuous ecstatic vision and was now fixed almost permanently in what psychologists refer to as "the immediate" or "awareness of now" and Eastern mystics call *mushin*—but without the discipline of focus. She had no basic skills appropriate for the twentieth century beyond those of a burnt-out seer. She was reaching for the door of the psychiatric hospital's schizophrenic ward. Fortunately her father was wealthy enough to keep her out of the hospital permanently, but she was unlucky enough to attract enough attention to get locked up from time to time (wailing and running through the streets covered with garbage and ashes attracts the wrong kind of attention for a girl trying to find god, even in a major American city).

Now in her thirties, she is coming to terms with her experience of the godhead and her lack of skills appropriate to survival in the material world. She paid for the four years of bliss with eighteen years of clinical depression and borderline psychosis. She is still attracted to mysticism and Native American religion, and has difficulty holding on to a job due to concentration problems. (We are hard on our saints and god-possessed in the material West.) Her story is more interesting than many and makes Gopi Krishna appear a piker of punishment. As she struggles to recover and attain a positive viewpoint, it is hoped that she will begin to write.

In the early nineties, researchers found that THC and anandamide bound to the same proteins in brain cells and occurred naturally in the brain as well as in marijuana. In the mid-nineties researchers found that the brain makes a second THC-like compound, sn-2 arachidonylglycerol, or 2-AG. The brain makes lots of this, and it affects energy levels and memory. Interestingly enough to me, if not to them, it is also found in the intestines, spleen, and pancreas, which are also sites having cannabinoid receptors. Kali, the Indian goddess associated with guerrilla warfare and the tantric arts, whose young and beautiful aspect acts as *dakini* to the kundalini, is also associated positively with marijuana. The cannabinoid sites are all organs associated with the inner fire and wisdom chakra. The Chinese will execute an opium or cocaine addict, but marijuana is a staple in many of their concoctions that have been in pharmaceutical use for thousands of years.

Stories like Lisa's are common if you do a little research with the Kundalini Resource Center (http://aloha.net/~bpeay/kundalini/index.html), or get down with El Collie and other wounded survivors of "bein' God teched" who contribute to her newsletter *Shared Transformations*, out of Sun Chariot Press, PO Box 5562, Oakland, CA 94605.

Pete is a well-read preacher's kid grown into a stable family man. He has been following my suggestions for a few years, as the following e-mail describes.

> The story of being attacked that I mentioned was kind of strange because I was not even really meditating. I had stalled on my chi kung and decided to just relax a little and build my

cave. I had been keyed up and was getting energy rushes all evening—tingling feelings, chills running my spine. I call it "feeling my skin." I had sent up a tall spired ceiling like the rotunda in Washington, with book shelves lining the walls to the top. I was picturing the doors, their various attributes, and then a giant spider appears and spears me with a leg right through my chest. I didn't get upset except the feelings intensified and I could feel every hair on my body—fear reaction maybe, but I thought I stayed pretty calm considering. A silk spider, I think. I looked it up. She carries a male on her back very small compared to her. He knows to stay away from her mouth lest he be eaten. I then slid sideways off the leg and fell on to the spider's back putting out the most benevolent and loving feelings I could. I got a general feeling of acceptance. I was then showered with a lot of smaller spiders crawling all over me. One of them bit me in the right palm and I watched as my nerves, or vessels, or something was covered with a black encasement. No ill effects from it. Everyone in the house got the flu except me, and the four-year-old. Pretty cool.

I didn't think I would be visited while working so close to home. I hadn't expected to see a spider, nor be attacked. Now I get visits from a dark-haired woman even when I'm not meditating. I can't see her very clearly. The ceiling of my cave is filled with webs, but now I'm not sure if it's just my imagination or wishful thinking. In any case I don't dare take them down. I thought your influence might have added to this vision, you being a spider and all.

I haven't made any progress with the chi kung yet. I'm a pretty subtle person. My kids can feel me when I try to feed them some energy, like when they are sick. I used to dump energy into my wife while we were going to sleep when she was pregnant. She never felt anything. I would always get a kick or some movement. She would make me move my hand because it annoyed her. The oldest is the most sensitive. She had the flu and when I came home I put my hand on her head trying to boost her up a little. She made me stop so I just let my fingers lay pointing at her forehead and focused on that. She kept telling me to stop. She's only five and wasn't looking at me, nor I at her. I usually can't feel my energy unless fed by strong emotion, "feeling my skin." It's hard to know if I'm doing it right as I am self-taught using yours and others directions. Well that's a little of my weirdness. I have adjusted pretty well to the new found psychosis. I had a Crisis Intervention Social Worker tell me I am a functional psychotic. I was a little worried about that label, but he said it wasn't bad. I never thought of my self in those terms. I am very good at de-escalation.

P. V. is an e-mail acquaintance who shares this little nugget.

While meditating several weeks ago with full and vigorous chi circulation flowing, I was visited by a very large bat. Normally I crush or swat visions, however I was intrigued. This is most unusual because I truly hate all rodents and have a particular dislike for bats. At any rate the bat found a perch on my face.

After a while, it began biting my nose and attacking my ears with its wings. My feeling was that it was trying to break the da chiao connection. At this point I am confused as to why I let it continue. Seeing I was not going to break da chiao, it then f——d my nose. After a while, I felt a swelling in the back of my throat (the bat was still on my face). I was still unwilling to break da chiao, and noticed some stuff starting to flow out of the right corner of my mouth to form a large, three-inch square cube, which I perceived as a diamond at the time. The diamond stood suspended next to my face until my meditation was complete and the bat disappeared. The next morning, there were numerous very small puncture wounds all around my nose.

Any help concerning the interpretation of this event is greatly appreciated.

The bat is the yin side of bird. Since you hate rodents it is appropriate that your shadow side familiar should be a bat. You can use your fetch to bring you toys from the void or ride it to places you want to visit. Your bat loves you and demonstrates its affection. You in turn demonstrated your diamond-hard resolution to keep observing rather than fighting or withdrawing. The diamond is formed from sexual energy. If you want the bat to be your buddy, and you should, feed it sexual energy or *chi*. The bat is a connection to the angels and goddesses of yin. The wounds are a stigmatic reminder of the dangers of psychosomatic alliances. A similar adventure led to my riding the great spider out into the web.

Another way of interpreting this vision is your familiar is trying to warn you that if you continue to follow the diamond sutra path you are f——d. Or it may be saying you are already too f——d-up to develop the diamond-hard consciousness of the *yidam* so the moment will not hold but fade away no matter how desperately you master the bated breath. If those two don't feel right, it is probably the first.

No matter how it all turns, you really have to take your shadow/familiar out more! It needs to develop a tidge more sophistication. Its a bit raw, and doesn't show much respect. Hatsumi-soke told me all the colors exist in black as well as white; you just have to be more sensitive to the light within the dark. Don't ignore, but stroke your bat.

From: Howard A. Davis, harimau@ccwf.cc.utexas.edu

To: spider1@firstnethou.com

Hey Dr. Morris,

Nicole says Hi and sends her love. I finally have a few minutes that allow me to provide you with some of the Toda meditation stuff. I am going to take a few days off. By the way, thanks for the advice on licensure. As usual, you're right and I am not looking far enough ahead again. I have an interesting supervisor. He's a Mason . . . both of you have a bit in common, I think. He is teaching me about the job much in the same ways that you teach me about life. No quarter given, no excuses accepted, and no idiocy allowed. I have to think and try to figure things out before I'll get an answer. It's interesting how I seem to be finding these folks in my life now. Oh, and Toda-san has me on a new diet. Mostly rice and a lot of sushi. He said it's to clean me out spiritually as well as physically. I am not sure of what he means but I think you'll understand more when you read what I have so far. So, without further ado, Heeeeeere's Toda!

Lessons from a Long Dead Grandmaster, a Testament from the Black Tiger (Howard A. Davis)

The Way is in Training. That is what all the ancients and the Masters say. Dr. Morris tells me the same thing when I am frustrated and whining about a lack of progress. Hakkeyoi means keep going, he says in his own inimitable way of a one-line e-mail or two if I am being exceptionally dense and whiny. So I kept going, on and off, meditating and training, practicing the sanshin and the kihon happo and working on my sitting kung, doing my reading and learning, always learning. Trying to make a pattern of things so that I don't stop. But, like all things in life, graduate school (the Master's of Science in Social Work program at the University of Texas at Austin), papers (which I love), classes (which are fun) stress (which SUCKS! but that's grad school), and politics (welcome to being an adult!) keep getting in the way. Or so I allowed myself to believe.

Oy! Was I frustrated, confused, and hungry for something, anything to happen in these damned meditations. This, I discovered later, is normal and a positive sign. Now, I needed to learn to quit working so hard. An old lesson from many a bugeisha and many an instructor in my life: when you stop trying and just do, things become effortless and things start to happen. Just "let go and relax into it" as Evil Shidoshi Dave says, as Dr. Morris says, as Hatsumi-soke says, as Dave Lowry and his instructor say, as Takuan Soho and Musashi say, as Jesus, and Buddhas say, etc. etc.

The Great Learning

So, like all those who went before me, I learned to relax and quit chasing clouds. My first experience in meditation was to discover my old meditation rest place inside of me where dwelt me, my True Self. It was a mess, no longer a clean bower of trees, with a clearing by a clear and cool stream in which I used to swim, and a crystal clear pool by which I used to sit and meditate. Some of the trees were very ill, some near death (a BAD sign). The water was murky and dark! It looked like old, dried blood. Little did I realize at the moment that it was a representation of just that. I, the True Me, was dying inside and polluting myself to death. I had to clean it up. It was not easy, I found many things there that I did not like. Visualization ain't always fun, warm and fuzzy! It took time, three months of work and sweat, and effort to clean up and to reestablish my rest place as a place where I could be. I found that each item there, and all the things that were wrong, were so because of negative experiences I had not processed and had accepted into my psychological make-up. I was killing myself to become something I am not, that something is "normal" just like everyone else. That's a hard bone to chew. I am different, always was, and I will always be. I set out to walk the Path of a bugeisha and I must remain there because my moral beliefs, my knowledge of self, my understanding and perceptions of what IS. Not many people like that. Our society, all societies in general in this modern age, prefer what we WANT things to be, over what they ARE in reality. The fantasy and fiction are SO much better than the reality.

So I cleaned it up and returned it to a place where I wanted to be. So much for being like everyone else. I am as unique as every other person and bugeisha in this world. Do the math, it ain't all that hard to figure out .

As this was happening, things were going smoothly, the fall semester of my first year was coming along fine. I met Dr. Morris off and on, he introduced me to (or is that gave me over to?) Evil Shidoshi Dave Bolin to teach me some of his magic and I became a part of an incredible family of ninja. I love them all. Hi Rich, got any more bruises for me? They all had something to share about love, support, faith, strength, different perspectives, trust, and more things that I can relate here. Dr. Morris was teaching me something by doing this. I am still working it out. Mostly, I think he was showing me that I am not the only one on the Path who walks it in this way. A surprise was waiting for me one Saturday night after a wonderful day of bump and grind with my new family and Dr. Morris. They had been pumping energy into me and getting me all filled up. Little did I know how that energy would affect me.

An Unexpected Visit

I went home that night and was meditating. I was in my little rest place, all nice and clean now, all my fears chased out (pushed away and hidden under the bed, if you will), and I was just sitting and resting. I heard some voices and look up, I was in the Void. Surprise surprise! I had unknowingly, and with no effort from myself, entered the Void. Here was a vision of Vishnu (a Hindu God) and a Buddha of Gold. Both kept shifting and never remained quite the same as they were when I looked at them before the shift. It's hard to explain. Imagine your cat or dog changing colors and fur patterns as you watch them. Makes you dizzy and that's what it was like. Never the same, always in flux and changing.

The Buddha and Vishnu were talking about me. It was interesting so I tried to get involved in their discussion. They would look over at me like I was some rude child, staring until I fell silent and then would return to their conversation. It was annoying to say the least. I started to think I was imagining them and that I had visualized them. The more I believed that, the louder they became in their conversation and the more they would give me that "idiot but loved child" look that parents get right before you get talked to about something really naughty. Finally, I accepted that they were real and I became more polite toward them (a good idea I later found out). As I became more appropriate, they sat, still in their conversation about me being lazy and undisciplined, in such a manner as to let me know I was now allowed to sit with them. Not to speak, only to listen, but allowed to sit with them. An interesting time. Unfortunately, I was not strong enough to remain and as I came out of meditation, they both smiled at me in a way that said they knew me, were watching me, and that I would one day get there. Wherever "there" was! I called Dr. Morris the next day and talked to him about it. He's my mentor, I am supposed to do that, remember?

Dr. Morris asks me questions about them, coloring, clothing, did they always look the same, stuff like that. I answer them honestly, believing what I now question at times. It was real and they were there. Oooh! A breakthrough. I got so excited I dove into meditation all full of expectation. A loss, complete and total. Too much effort. It has never happened again. Lazy and undisciplined. They were right.

The Dead Grandmaster

Thanks to Dr. Morris, Dave, and Rich, I have experienced many things, opening of chakras, the third eye opening while driving, a crystal shop in Austin causing weird sensations and playing havoc with my energy, learning that I can become depressed and suicidal when life kicks me in the teeth over and over again, but that I can get up and keep going. Discovering that there are those folks who love and care for me without having a request for me to reciprocate. Dr. Morris came to Austin to visit with my wife (Nicole, she's an amazing woman!) and I to get away from Houston and to get me back on track with my own life. He helped me pull out of a peculiarly dangerous time. It was scary but he helped me see and correct my perceptions of things. Undying devotion and a BIG giri there.

In all of this there is Learning, always learning, that the key in making life work right is in relationships (get the hint here or suffer untold agonies, Kihon Happo, ukemi, good lesson about this). Well, because I was trying to get back into it again and working hard with Wild Ricky (one of my Houston ninja brothers), I had a wonderful thing happen out of the blue.

Again, I had calmed myself, and my life down, to a point where I could begin again on getting the kundalini released (a task not yet accomplished to this day, no schedule and pattern). After a few days, I again slid back into effortless meditation. For some time, I had felt someone had been watching me, a feeling that I had been getting constantly, and that someone was waiting for me in my rest place. He was dead. I mean really dead. We're talking near one hundred years dead. He was Takamatsu-san's grandfather and instructor. It was Toda Shinryuken Masamitsu. Oh did I freak out when I learned that bit. It has been an experience. He talked to me and hugged me as best he could. He encouraged me to keep training and told me that I was back on the Path where I BELONGED. That I have the ability but no discipline and that he would help me if I would allow it. I had just been offered the keys to heaven for a bujinkan student. I was being offered to become the pupil of one of our grandmaster's. Talk about happy. I had no idea.

I have had many meetings with Toda-sama and he has spoken with me many times. He comes and goes as he feels I need it. He recently came to me in a meditation session (I still have no pattern or schedule developed thanks to life). I relaxed into it without quite thinking about it and drifted into the Void. A nice place to be. The darkness carries a warmth to it, a familiarity and comforting feeling. Here comes Toda-sensei, smiling and wearing a bright orange shinobi-zue (ninja uniform, if you will). He looks like a Buddhist monk from bad Shaolin movies. He smiles, hugs me, leans over to my ear, cups his hand around it and yells at the top of his lungs, "YOU ARE LAZY AND UNDISCIPLINED!" Toda-soke tells me, "You think too much and then not enough, you confuse desires and wants, for needs and necessities." Whoa, what a greeting. "You are a disgrace to our lineage and to our family that I, and others, worked hard to develop and build and nurture to this state. But, you are ours and this shall soon change." Another smile, enigmatic as always. It turns out that he meant that I am without self-control and that I will not go through the pain and discomfort necessary to change my lifestyle. An interesting statement from beyond. The dead have ways of getting our attention, it seems. Much as the Gods. It ain't always comfy and friendly and loving. Or so it seems to us as the recipients.

Toda-soke had spoken to me before about my training and gave me a precise schedule to follow and obey. I had not done this for more than two weeks before I stopped due to my constantly shifting life. Again, grad school strikes. The pattern of activity he advocated parallels the manner in which tai chi instructors I have since spoken with direct their classes on nei kung (energy work) and meditation. Toda-san had told me to first work on sanshin, slowly and cautiously, watching my breathing and balance. Second, to move into kihon happo with or without my partner and ninja brother Ricky, and to watch distance and timing. THEN move to meditation. I was told to do this twice daily, once in the morning at five A.M. and meditate by six A.M. And then in the evening, after I got home. It seems that the Tai Chi Sifu and SiGung (who also is a marvelous Hung Gar stylist, Master Moses Williams, Jr. of Austin's The Fire Dragon Martial Arts Institute) advocate the same thing. Start with nei kung, move to tai chi, and then to meditation. The reason is for blood and breath circulation and energy development BEFORE meditation. Interesting how a dead Japanese soke would impart that to me. Again, a question of being too lazy to do the research and finding out in the time that the cosmos decides. I did as he had told me for a while but again, let my world dictate my actions and thoughts rather than remaining in control. I accepted a passive place of victimization. How comfortable it is to return to what we know rather than to change and survive the discomfort of change. So Toda-soke's comment about lazy and undisciplined is too true to hear.

I have been training daily now and I feel the shift in my perceptions again, I feel my breathing coming easier. My insight in my professional life (*haragei*, and it is seriously important in my line of work) has sharpened and improved. I can empathize with clients because I can feel, and at times, touch their emotions. I have greater faith in myself and in my abilities. And my rest place is getting brighter and greener. Nothing huge yet but I can sense a difference after three weeks of serious training according to a schedule. I am more able to sense and see patterns—a plus as a therapist. And I realize that I am not all-powerful, correct at all times, or perfect in anything. My walk has changed, my mind works more sharply, and I need less sleep. I feel my energy running up and down my spine and I can't slouch when I sit anymore. Good posture in oneself brings about interesting and respectful behaviors and reactions from those around you. I carry myself with more confidence. All this after only three weeks. The way IS in training.

All of this has taught me a few things. One, that when you find Truth, pay attention to it. We all have a tendency to keep seeking the hard stuff, and if I wish to, all I have to do to get to my goal is listen to my teachers and learn from their mistakes. Two, we can learn from just about anyone, but especially teachers and parents. The elders have some good ideas, good advice, if we'll just shut up and listen. Third, most of what is out there can be found if you read. But, most of all, that if I want the results and wish to be something, that I have to work at it. Live it every day at all moments. Nothing is instant, each seed grows in its own time. There's no point in rushing it. Sifu, how right you were.

From: Smakmykrak@aol.com

To: spider1@firstnethou.com

I don't know anything about anything, so I don't know how it computes at all. I was feeling nervous, overwhelmed by changes in myself and my job, working with a therapist. So he said, "Let's go inside and find out what is making you feel so nervous." He usually interprets nervousness as energy that I need to channel correctly, unless something else comes up like a subpersonality that needs a little attention. So he has me do a relaxation thing and go to my favorite spot, which is under a big tree in the grass. He says, Ask whatever it is that is making you feel this way to join you there. An image comes up and I converse with it, communicate with it, or if it's just energy it still has an image. I see where the blow is and soften it. This time a black lady with at least six arms and tusks came popping into my space and surprised me. She was kinda ugly so I was like "Whoa." Then she said "Oh don't let me scare ya honey" in an ethnic accent. I asked why she came, she said to help me get motivated and get things done. A little more conversation and I thanked her for coming and helping, and was there anything she needed from me? She said, "I could use a cigarette . . . and a hair brush if you got one." So I laughed! She was so funny, reminded me of Nell Carter. During our talk she started to change into a Donna Summers-looking person with many arms and sequined dress. She had the same wit and spark, and an energy that made me giggly. She said I could call on her if I needed her and waved good-bye with each arm.

My symptoms haven't changed much, but I'm not so horny anymore. I still heat up now and then. The swaying is more prominent if I meditate with my tongue down. Things look more 3-D sometimes. The ringing is still in my ears, but seems to be moving more to my right ear. It was in my left before.

I had a terrible dream last night. I found two of my dogs gutted and feet cut off in the backyard of my old house. As the police were investigating, my dogs became reanimated and walked over to me to kiss me and say good-bye. This morning I said to them, "I'm glad you still got guts." As I said it I noticed it sounded like I was saying "Glad you're still brave." The whole thing was weird, I usually love my dreams. And with this one no matter how many times I woke or how long I stayed awake I still kept going back into it all night.

Warrior by definition? I don't know if I am, or what is, but it seems like I have had to fight to stay alive or sane all my life, so I feel like one. Maybe I'm a warrior reincarnated? That would be cool!!! You said Kali is a death goddess? If you can make sense of any of this, please do. I don't think I'm ready to die yet, things are just getting good. May be it will finally be the death of this ego, and I can grow up.

Personal Notes

Close to Christmas 1997 my mother had her final stroke and at eighty-four was paralyzed, blind, and mute, but would not die. I left my body for a few trips to prepare a place, do some bargaining, then visited her in the spirit world. (She had been my father's keeper for the last ten years, and even had my sister fooled to the extent of his Alzheimer's damage. He forgets at a frightening rate.) She was dying in Florida and I was in Houston. It didn't take me too long to convince her that she had completed her work and could do no more for Daddy or us in this life, in that body. She died peacefully, in no pain, but will be sorely missed as she was a great and kindly woman proud of her children's accomplishments, and the depth of the gene pool was her side. We were fortunate that she had made a living will and it was enforced.

Without her, the love of his life and helpmate of over sixty years, like a swan Dad will follow her into the void. She was a great beauty in her youth. A flapper fox into math and skepticism. Never content in her role of "the preacher's wife," she always held a job, and taught in the local schools wherever we lived. She took her joy in books, and was shy. Her corpse was so cold. I have wept daily for a month at my own loss, and the brute grief I feel in Dad, which he cannot express as he cannot remember why he is alone in a foreboding landscape different from the mountains of Pennsylvania. He does not remember the last fifteen years of retirement. What goes around, comes around.

146

Mom, on the other hand, is rested and happy with the library and interesting surroundings in her new residence. I'm sure she will adjust to the demon servants quickly. She can do the math.

My son sent a copy of his doctoral dissertation in chemistry for Christmas. What a treat! I don't understand a word of it. He had recently resigned from an extremely well-paid corporate post-doctorate head of laboratory position so his fiancee could return to California to finish her medical schooling. He was very quickly picked up by the government willing to pay a GS 13 for his expertise. In the dissertation he had written the following:

> Dad, I give you a lot of credit for where I am today. I still remember the day in junior high school when you sat me down and detailed out how depressing my future would be if I didn't start using my brain. I can't list all the things you have done for me. All I can say is thanks, and that I love you. Dr. Shawn H. Phillips.

I wish I could remember what I said to him back then. I would bottle it. My older daughters, Teri Dawn and Tamarah, are presenting me with grandsons and I have a feeling an iron fist will be necessary to curb them (the grandsons), because the girls were never much into discipline. Fortunately I am too old to care, and will have my own problems in abundance by the time I would have to step into theirs.

Anu is a college student in California who has been plaguing me with e-mail questions concerning techniques for a couple of years. At my suggestion Anu studies *budo taijutsu* with *shidoshi* Dale Seago in San Francisco. Recently she sent me the following.

> This is a poem I wrote after my first "weird" experience with the kundalini and some of my feelings that I felt then (if only they lasted!). Need for competition and need for approval has always plagued me, and this glimpse pointed to a change from that. I'm not much of a poet, but I thought I'd share it:

An Angle on Angels

I asked to see an angel,
And instead I see a beast
But how unusual a beast!
Eyes like stars, such a tranquil and magnanimous face
Soft light exudes from him with an iridescent, holy glow
Beast like? In appearance, perhaps; but certainly not in demeanor
Uninhibited to be sure,
But his natural urges and instincts are divine
He feels no lack, no small-heartedness
No battle within himself, no separate, contrary selves
No disintegrated movements of mind
His motivation is pure like brilliant crystal
Blinding in its splendor, unassailable in its integrity
His nature and grace are beautiful like the spring flowers
His spirit hard and clear like a diamond
Love emanates from his heart, filling his body to the very skin
And it radiates out, touching all around him
Blessing and making whole
Spreading life to a dying, blighted world

—Anuragh Mehta

CHAPTER ELEVEN

Chi *Sickness*

Conformity is the jailer of freedom and the enemy of growth.

> John F. Kennedy, errant husband, assassinated president, speech to United Nations, 1961

Though God hath raised me high, yet this I count the glory of my crown: that I have reigned with your loves.

> Elizabeth I, great monarch,
> *The Golden Speech,* 1601

"C'est la nuit qu'il est beau croire a la lumière. (It is at night that faith in light is admirable.)

> Edmond Rostand, poet and playwright,
> *Chantecler,* 1907

Bioelectrical Phenomena

Chi cleansing and *chi* sickness are synonymous, rather like the flushing out of toxins one experiences with many herbal remedies. I put out a request on the Internet about a year ago for people to share their experiences. As you can imagine, some were rather tripish (derived from tripe, not trip) and lacked certain details that made me doubt the credibility of the author. Below are the ones that appealed to my sense of humor and circumspection. I don't always identify the writer for various reasons but can verify that I have seen or experienced events relatively close to what they describe.

A middle-aged, unabashedly conservative, WASP geologist from Denver writes,

> Began studies in several of the martial arts several times but this is the only time I've stuck with it for more than a few weeks. I like budo taijutsu. I've been in more physical confrontations than most people. Probably because the people that I work around are full-blown psychopaths. I work as a consultant in the oil patch most of the time. Also do some consulting in the construction and mining industries. I don't know the why of why I'm writing. Have only read your first book, and am still trying to figure out if you are for real or not.
>
> Before I tried your techniques re: *chi* development and the Secret Smile, I studied somewhat to see what I might be getting into. I found a book entitled *chi* kung by some Chinese guy who described the hazards of improper use and development of the *chi*. On reading this book, I realized that I had been doing this for almost thirty years and didn't know the name for it. I thought that everyone did this. I decided that further exploration was warranted.
>
> Continuing with *chi* development, I decided to apply this to repair of my right shoulder damaged from a fight long ago, five years playing rugby, competitive swimming and racquetball. Several orthopedists have strongly cautioned against surgical repair because the risk of greater injury is very high.

Chi *Sickness*

I had full circulation going and directed most of the *chi* to the injured spot. Whereon my right arm began shaking spasmodically. I started laughing and kept sending the energy to the injury until I was tired. My arm kept shaking, I kept laughing. It didn't seem to help, but it was kind of fun.

A while later, I described the situation to one of the students that I train with. This fellow had previously studied iron hand kung fu. He immediately diagnosed the problem as a *chi* "leak." With this new information, I again directed the *chi* to the shoulder but closed my arm to prevent the leakage. The situation that developed was far less funny and resulted in a massive, painful contraction of my chest. I thought that I might be having a heart attack. Unable to move my arm, I was able to reduce the energy flow and think that I have recovered. This was about a week ago. My conclusion is that *chi* development and application is probably not the sort of thing that should be written about for general, untrained public consumption. I have little doubt that I could have died.

Obviously, I must have been deriving benefit to have persevered through these tribulations. The benefit that I most appreciate is the renewal of physical and psychic energy resulting from, as you say, "running the meridians." The benefit that I believe to be greatest is my renewed association with my God. This is in the US traditional sense of the word. Preceding or antecedent (is this a word?) my meditations with prayer result not only in a tremendous mystical understanding of oneness, but also of knowing that I am where I am supposed to be today—of knowing that this is not where I am supposed to be tomorrow, or where I was supposed to have been yesterday, and forgiveness. The sixth benefit is a better understanding of the power available in the universe. What I am continuing to be confused about is our (humanity's) place in the universe.

A Victorian Canadian *ninja* writes,

It was 1995. I had been training and helping to teach about six days a week. I would run down to the dojo, six miles there, and then walk back home kinda tired after two hours of training. From somewhere in your Path Notes book I picked up the idea that I should breathe with my stomach so I trained myself whenever I could to use the diaphragm.

Well lucky me, my wish came true! One weeknight I came home from the dojo and went to bed. Then went to the toilet, both ends. Now I'd spent four years in the Canadian Navy, and I can get seasick with the best of them, but I have never had such a violent, wrenching spewfest as that night. Seven times I grappled with the porcelain god.

I made a small cot for myself in the living room so I wouldn't wake my roommates, and continued to amuse myself. I had no clue and little warning as to what was happening. The pain in the guts was similar to the kenjutsu techniques where you slide past uke and twist the saya around in his obi, although more intense and localized in my stomach.

After the first VomeEx (Canadian naval term for vomiting) I had no wish to eat or drink other than to get rid of the taste of bile. After about the third time I was getting concerned about dehydrating so I began to drink juice. Over the next three days I was laid up by this amazing bout of what had to have been *chi* sickness although I wouldn't know. I'm not an expert yet.

During the next day the vomiting subsided to about half the frequency of the night before. The second night maintained the same frequency, and again for the third day. The third night was quiet and I ate food for the first time on the morning of the fourth day. By the fifth day I was back at work and training.

To this day I breathe with my stomach, and I find it helps in my cardiovascular abilities and keeping me healthy. The juice continued to replenish lost electrolytes. Today I would switch with half fresh juice and half sport drinks (Gatorade or whatever). I believe I will get a chance to try this juice therapy out as I continue to advocate stomach breathing to my students.

Chi *Sickness*

Jason Sowell, a *shodan* in *bujinkan* and red belt in *hoshin* under Frank Hagen who attended my seminars in Florida at Greg Cooper's *dojo,* reports the following after attending the Earth Seminar.

I first saw Dr. Morris at Greg's house where we were staying. We had a beer. Friday night he taught a traditional ninjutsu class without meditation, just good thump and bump. Saturday and Sunday were the Earth seminar. It was going to be the esoteric mixed with the combat stuff for two days out of the base chakra. My experience of *chi* sickness did not start until Saturday morning, when we started to work with the different forms of earth energy (bear strikes) and differing meditations. After about thirty minutes, I began to feel a little bit sick and lightheaded. Not bad at first, just a little off-balance. The feeling grew until we broke for lunch. When we went to the sub shop, I knew I was sick and decided to only drink a little Sprite.

After sitting in the sub shop for a few minutes, I wanted to be out in the fresh air. I went back to the dojo and sat down on the curb. Now my head was hurting, a dull, throbbing pain, and I felt like I was hungover. Some time into this feeling I lost all my Sprite in a quick projectile spew. After this I began to sip my Sprite, sat down against the wall, started pulling the energy down from my head keeping my tongue up, and swirling it toward my hara. That was all I could think to do at the time. After doing this for a while I felt better, so I got up and went back into the dojo. Big mistake!

Inside the dojo, it was just in time to get caught up in another meditation. I felt like my head was expanding outward with this new influx of energy. I was able to sit down, kept drawing this energy down to the hara, and practiced some more swirling exercises. This kept me from getting sick again, which was also helped by having an empty stomach.

When the seminar was over for the day, we went back to Coop's home. I felt better; it was cool inside and I took a shower. Then we all went to dinner. Bigger mistake!

We went to a nice Italian restaurant. At dinner I was feeling OK so I ordered a simple dish of noodles with tomato sauce. I was not affected by the sight of food but the smell just blew me away. I felt like I had the flu combined with a hangover. I left the table and went to the rest room. I stood in a stall and got the urge to vomit under control. It was funny but I really liked the cool air and the smell of the deodorants. After awhile, being away from the smell of food, I started feeling better.

After thirty minutes or so, I went outside and walked around. I still had to avoid the food smells but was able to drink a little Sprite. After everyone finished dinner we went home. One of the other guys couldn't eat either, and he went to collapse in his car. During the party that went on at Coop's I began to feel better, became ravenous, ate my meal and drank a lot of fruit juices. The funny thing was the way this sickness came on me and then left me. It was like someone was flipping a switch. On the drive back to Tennessee I had light attacks of sickness that backed down when I swirled and drank more juice.

Well, that's my first experience of *chi* sickness, it probably won't be the last. I did give this some thought (very dangerous), and came to the conclusion that if Hatsumi-soke was sick for eighteen months and Greg was sick for nine months and both seem to have more sense than I do, I figure that I will only be sick for nine hours. Sounds good to me.

Shidoshi-ho Greg Cooper, whom I've known since his white belt days back in the early eighties when we were both attending Stephen Hayes's seminars, is now one of the better teachers of traditional *budo taijutsu*. He spent three or four years living in Japan and gets back as often as he can to try to keep up with the Boss's new direction. He is fluent in Japanese, has a degree in Eastern Religious Studies, and has a better understanding of tantra than most of the thugs in this game. His wife Gina has accompanied him on many of his adventures. Here's his story.

Chi *Sickness*

My first experience with energy work was at a seminar given by Duncan Callister in the early eighties. This was also the first time I met Dr. Morris. Duncan performed a healing on me in which I felt an incredibly strong current of energy pass from his hands to mine and then through my body into the earth. This washed away some emotional baggage I had been carrying for a few years and afterward I felt totally cleansed. It was like I had received a spiritual enema. For a few weeks afterward I was all mellow, forgiving, and Christlike. Then reality crept back in on little clawed feet. Duncan treated Glenn like a peer and they would occasionally wander off from the group exercises and do strange things that the rest of us could not see but felt.

After this seminar and on Glenn's recommendation, I began reading anything I could find on tantra and all of Mantak Chia's Healing Tao publications. As an aside, at twenty-two years of age I thought seminal retention was the craziest thing I'd heard. Now at thirty-one, it makes me feel eighteen again. [It still has that effect on me at fifty-four, and from watching the Boss I would guess that sixty-eight ain't too bad either.] Anyway, I began a sporadic practice of *chi* kung as a twenty-two year old with a lot of distractions.

In the fall of 1993 my wife Gina and I had been living in Japan for almost two years. I was working too much and every spare moment was spent in the dojo training. I had no time for rest and no relaxing place to go short of Hawaii. I had bitten off more than I could chew. On the positive side I was getting to train with the Boss and various shihan two and three times a week. Naguchi for flow, Shiraishi for details and groundwork, Muramatsu for fighting, Ishazuka for power, and the Boss for creativity, or at least that is how I saw it. I was also meditating religiously every night, no matter how exhausted I was from being thrown about by these various paragons of ninja power.

One night while meditating, I felt the energy building dangerously high. I tried to back it down, but it was too late. My kidney caps opened up and dumped a load of adrenaline into my system, setting off a full-fledged panic attack. I knew I needed to ground the energy but was unable to concentrate or relax enough to do so. I ran around our tiny apartment like the proverbial headless chicken. Prior to this I had no trouble eating, though I did have occasional diarrhea that I attributed to stress and new bugs. After this night I could only eat fruit and bland foods. The smell of grease and soy sauce would make me ill. I had constant diarrhea, which was made worse by having to use Japanese squat toilets most of the time. I survived on orange juice and onigiri [little rice balls wrapped in seaweed].

I went to many doctors who could give me no better diagnosis than gastritis [Latin for irritable stomach]. They gave me gobs of horse pills and sent me on my way. I tried kampoyaku, a Chinese herbal medicine that helped for a while but then made things worse. I tried an American treatment for irritable bowel syndrome that had nasty side effects and didn't work. We were beginning to think we would not survive to the end of our English school contracts. In June of 1994 I had an endoscopy performed at St. Luke's Hospital in Tokyo. Again no organic problems were found. After this the irritable bowel syndrome abated somewhat but I still felt lightheaded. Gina began to think we would never enjoy going out to a good restaurant again and she would spend the rest of her life eating yogurt and rice balls.

The only time I felt normal during this period was in training. Training allowed me to concentrate on something other than my body going haywire. I also stopped meditating because I thought that was the source of my problem. I lost a lot of weight that did not return until I was back in the States eating my mother-in-law's fine Italian home-cooking.

I know now that I should have kept meditating. I should have gone to an acupuncturist instead of allopathic doctors. So much for 20/20 hindsight. This was the longest and harshest period of *chi*-sickness that I experienced. Every subsequent episode was milder and easier to control. Of course, the neural rewiring continues today. The period leading up to the heart chakra was unnerving. During the late summer and early fall of 1995, I was constantly aware of the beating of my heart. I would have anxiety attacks and palpitations while waiting in lines or while stopped at red lights. My vision would flicker like strobe lights and do other strange things. I continued to meditate during this period and it helped me accept and control the weirdness. When the heart chakra opened, I again experienced that feeling of universal love and oneness that I had felt with Callister, and since Glenn and I were now friends I would call him about my symptoms. This time I didn't feel so Christlike, but felt a greater empathy toward Shirley McClaine.

Now when my students tell me of the strange things that happen to them I laugh long and hard. Then I reassure them that it is all part of the ride and its best to relax, keep smiling, and enjoy the trip. It does help to have friends that have gone before you. It keeps you from panicking and running up a huge medical bill.

Karim abu Shakra is a computer wizard from Amman, Jordan. He was part of the original Hillsdale College *hoshinjutsu* group and now sets up computer networks for banks and various industries throughout the Middle East as an independent consultant.

hi morris . . . i am always happy to hear that my friends are doing well. . . .my best to you . . . my only *chi* story was in North Carolina. . . .the day before i left to amman. . . .summer '92 . . . i picked up a girl from a disco and went to her house. . . . for the rest of the night, i took her from one orgasm to another . . . i was fully clothed most of the time. . . . what was wild was that i was her orgasm . . . i commanded it. . . .i would bring her orgasm up with the touch of my fingers and it was not on her clit or anything . . . her arms, her chest, legs, torso . . . i would use circular motions. . . . with every revolution, i would draw her orgasm close until i decided it was time to explode it. . . . she was going crazy . . . totally out of it, and was in a state of confusion as to what was happening. . . . i was kind of amused and didn't really care for penetration or ejaculation . . . it was sufficient seeing her eyes beg for mercy. . . . i remember calling you the next day from the airport to tell you about it and you asked me if i brought the orgasm to her head. . . . at the time i didn't think of that, but as soon as you mentioned it, it made sense . . . so that is why the women like you so much.

Another interesting story happened to me in California . . . i was relaxing on a couch in my bedroom . . . second floor . . . outside was a water fountain that was always running. . . . i used the sound to sleep . . . that day i had worked hard and was just stretching down . . . decided to concentrate on the sound of falling water . . . soon i was in the fountain . . . i was wet and i touched myself and felt the water on my body . . . i was conscious throughout the experience . . . but the water level was rising in the fountain as i lay there motionless . . . i was aware that the water level was rising and began to fight it as it came closer to drowning me . . . i fought ferociously to snap out of it and i finally did . . . that scared the shit out of me . . . also i was never able to do that again. . . . i don't think this is related to *chi* but you make what you think of it. . . .it would help if you could explain. [I don't have a clue, old buddy, but as a mystic metaphor or Freudian dream your experience could be interpreted in a number of different directions.]

This is from a doctoral candidate from the number-one graduate school in physics in America. He studied *hoshintao chi kung* with me.

Hellooo, all,

Long time no communiqué. So, let's tell a story. The last two weeks, I've been turning up the quigong exercising, particularly some called "converting jing to *chi*" (semen into *chi*). They're really just preparatory exercises for opening the microcosmic orbit, but I look at it as lifting weights. I've just mixed them in with other things. Sometimes when I do them, I see a swirl of activity in the air over my lap, looking sort of like a pixie having fun. I lie down. Nowadays, my dreams seem to be over-flowing with sexual content, and I remember some of them after I wake up, throughout the day, seeing the eyes of the female(s) looking at me. There is one in particular who in retrospect reminds me of a vision I had in meditation last summer. Also, whenever I close my eyes to go to bed, I have visions. They're not quite as clear as they used to be, but I guess they'll clear up eventually. I've taken to always asking their name, their true face, and feeding them with my breath; I also usually take on the form of some handsome hulk; it seems to help with attracting the females.

Three nights ago, I contacted a female named Ishta or Ishtar. Her voice was very musical, and she was built. The next night, there was some wolflike being who wasn't too friendly. I forget his name, something with three syllables and starting with an M, but after I got on better terms with him and he started looking more human as I kept feeding him energy, there was a change, a female face appeared, and I again asked for a name, and she said Diana. Things weren't too clear for me, but with a full moon and a wolf-guard, I guess that was the Hunter; maybe not.

Last night, a male form appeared named Muktar, his voice like the Borg. I asked him what he needed. He said, "You."

I said, "Sorry, I need me too. Is there anything else I can give you? I'm still a bit clumsy with this energy exchange bit."

I just started breathing to him for a while, feeling the air suck into the palms of my hands and feet, and then out of my nose. I tried sending with my hands, and at first they were hot, but then they shifted to cold. I decided it was better that way anyway. Eventually, I communicated more, and then I saw a hand approaching with a little jeweled sword in its palm. Later came other things like a mace, etc. The poor guy got gypped, all I could think of giving was a few roses. Me and my roses. I have to figure out something better to give. These spirits haven't always been pretty, but I try to just give them food anyway. Eventually they change or I ignore them. Sometimes I just see an eye or eyes staring at me.

Yesterday when I came home, there was a butterfly on my door. Today, when I went to school, a butterfly appeared and landed on a pole near me. I tried communicating with it, and then a car passed by and it flew away. As I walked on, it caught up with me and landed on my shoulder.

I've been doing a little research for you on the esoteric meanings of spider stuff for the ancient Chinese. Rereading, back to references of spider chapter in Suntzu's Art of War. I read the original chapters 1–7 and 13 but not the others. Some guesses: if among what I read, is 13 or 6. However, last night I analyzed the chapter names, and the only one that comes close to it is Chapter 11. It literally means nine changes, but the character for change has silk strands in it. One analysis of this character is to see it as a spool of thread or "silk source" with two strands coming out (a node in a web?), and a word in between them (an image of speaking between the lines). An older form of the character has three strands rather than two strands a word. The newer form of the sub-unit with the strand-word-strand form basically means to argue. I didn't like the explanations as to why, but I would say its from two lines of thought and words exchanged between them, thus "conflict," but of course other meanings as well. One of the explanations I read was that, in trying to untie a knotty lock of threads, one emits expletives, thus to argue. Anyway, websource, strands, hidden meanings— esoteric spider. The character nine, in one of its oldest forms (it's on my watch), has the character for king in it. Ergo "spider prince."

The character for "dark, mysterious," as in the esoteric dark woman of the Daodejing [DDJ equals Tao Te Ching to us non-Chinese speaking knuckle-walkers], is a character few modern Chinese can explain. I'll tell you my analysis. The original character looks like an hourglass or the Roman numeral for 10, and, as I read in one of my dictionaries, is an image of two intertwined threads; they're not knotted together, they're just hooked or crossed over each other like a character X. Another image of this linking is that they form a double helix, and you're seeing a side perspective, thus an X (that's my interpretation). Seeing the threads as lines of thought or as "concrete ideas," two that seem real and sensible on their own (i.e., have and lack, form and formlessness, full and void). Yet when you try to reconcile them, they don't merge into a new concrete idea—the only way you can handle the complete idea is to play with the parts and try to understand the whole as best you can.

This analysis of the character not only fits the way it is used in the "first" poem of the Daodejing, but the first poem tries to make a point about the limitations of concrete thinking and verbal constructive pedagoguery. The first Westerner to say the same thing as eloquently was Godel with his Incompleteness Theorem. What I'm telling you is not something I read or was told, but my own thinking over the past year. The reason I mentioned this is that the image of the word between the lines is similar to the idea of two concrete yet irreconcilable lines of thought.

The first poem of the DDJ, which ends with "mystery upon mystery ... " uses this character and can be seen as an inductive model (n+1) symbolizing a whole web of these crossing threads. The web perhaps being a full one line or a ball of silk fuzz. This is also an image of the network connections among "gels," as in jello. We are jello. Our bodies are gells with cells.

The second point I wanted to make was about your friend the spider, an analysis of the Chinese name for spider. The special character for door is the same as the one found in the Japanese name "Togakure," and it has meanings like sect (literally a door unto teachings) and others. But door to esoterica is an obvious interpretation. Another translation of kumogakure could be the "spider hidden behind the clouds." Sun Tzu emphasizes seeing the truth and the character "to know" is a spider and also a "mouth shooting arrows" meaning words aimed with truth. Tatsu can mean dragon as well as "a man of standing." Jin can mean spirit of man. Tatsujin. Any stories you'd like to tell? Take care.

Breath Work in *Chi Kung* and Greek Orthodoxy

Breath in Chinese has metaphysical meanings as well as physical ones. It is common in Gong-style *shing-yi* to be told to move the breath to the palms, breathe through the kidneys, etc. This is obviously physically impossible and is due to the translation of *chi* as breath. Older *tai chi* manuals and current *chi kung* manuals discuss mixing the heaven and earth breath or five-gate breathing. The same problem is seen in other languages, especially in Greek. In *shing-yi chuan* and *hoshinroshiryu,* students are taught deep-belly breathing for beginners (natural breath), and once they are able to feel subtle energy, they are moved on to the reverse, or Taoist, breath. In Gong-style *shing-yi,* this is done as a specific exercise called teacup breathing, or the 100-breath exercise. This is taught to make students physically stronger and increase their ability to generate *chi.* Other patterns of physical breathing are used to cultivate the movement of the *chi.* Many schools of *chi kung* teach such techniques to some degree. However, as *shing-yi* teacher Tom Morrissey points out, in actual fighting the physical breath is always kept low. Sifu Kenny Gong would often describe moving the breath "from the ground" so that Mr. Morrissey would later explain that this did not mean you were supposed to suck air in through your feet! Hatsumi-soke recommends keeping the feet warm.

The misconceptions concerning breath and energy work probably originate from the fact it is physically possible to "breathe" in the reverse pattern, where breathing in through the foot appears so impossible that one instinctively looks for another meaning. The point of the Taoist breath in the seated meditations taught in the *hoshinroshiryu* is to move the *chi* up the back to eventually connect the genitals' energy to the brain (or in *shing-yi,* the *tan t'ien* to the brain), thus providing more energy and control. These techniques are common to most systems of medical *chi kung*. The baby breath is how babies breath! Adults have lost the knack and have to visualize to get it back. The perversions of proper breathing patterns used by more than a few *karate* systems may be practical jokes passed on by students who did not realize their teacher was pulling their legs. It also could be an attempt to harden the body and obtain the resistance to strikes that *chi kung* develops. Retaining energy and holding the breath are not similar, but a poor translation of an esoteric text may make them seem so. Master Cheng's *Thirteen Chapters on Tai-chi Chuan* is an excellent and extensive introduction to *chi-kung* and its applications.

The Orthodox churches, often referred to by the country they immigrated from to the United States, are a collection of churches under the historical Patriarchates of Christianity. Rome is one of these, but separated for theological and political reasons about a thousand years ago. The term "Orthodox" means right worship, and reflects the Orthodox concern with action as well as belief. Relations with the Roman Catholic Church can best be described as unpleasant. Unlike both Protestants, who accept only the Bible, and Catholics, who follow the teachings of the Pope, Orthodoxy (like a *ryu*) believes in a continuing tradition based on the consensus of the church over centuries. This means there is a strong emphasis on the writings of the fathers and a strong concern with original intent. Bible verses in the Orthodox method are not numbered to be individually extracted, as they are studied in context. As the Church chose the books collected into the Bible in the third and fourth centuries, Orthodox interpretations tend to depend on the writings of the early fathers, who were disciples of the Apostles and their successors.

In Orthodoxy every Christian is called to constantly and continually pray. The hesychastic movement developed from this concept and from the command, "Be still and know I am God" (Psalm 46:10). This is a simplification of an almost two-thousand-year-old monastic tradition, as the roots of it can be seen in the Essenes and in the New Testaments. The first flowering occurred in the fifth century A.D. in the Egyptian and Syrian desert, and it continues there today, as well as on Mount Athos in Greece, with a continuous tradition of over 1,500 years. The same can be seen in Valaam, in Finland (800 years or so), as well as at sites in Russia, Ukraine, Bulgaria, Romania, Lebanon, the Middle East, and also in the United States. A written as well as an oral tradition exists, and lines of teachers can be traced back centuries to people regarded as especially holy. The need for an experienced teacher—a spiritual father or mother—is emphasized because success is difficult without one. To quote Musashi once more, "You must make your warrior's walk your every day walk."

Hesychasm comes from the Greek meaning "to be quiet, at rest" and refers to a way of life that left the world for the silence of the desert. This movement started in the fourth century and continues today. A more specialized group of meaningful exercises were called by this term in the fourteenth century, when the monks of Mount Athos practiced a special type of prayer in addition to the other ascetic labors. The Roman Catholic Church, which split from The Eastern Orthodox Churches in the eleventh century, follows the opinion of Barlaam the Calabrian. Barlaam, later made a bishop of the Roman Church for his attacks on the Athonite monks, was the great opponent of the hesychast and coined the insulting term "omphaloskepsis," or "navel gazer," to mock them. "Navel gazing" is often used by martial artists today in a similar tone to mock internal practitioners.

The basic Orthodox meditative technique is part of what the Orthodox call the "Prayer of the Heart," and the physical techniques are a very small part of it. The prayer most often said is "Lord Jesus Christ, Son of God, have mercy on me, a sinner" is repeated first orally and then mentally until it becomes continual. The prayer works itself inward until the mind settles in the heart. The breathing and focusing techniques are used to facilitate this. The Orthodox practice is similar to how I teach the use of secular affirmations or the assumption of attitudes that correspond to chakra or endocrine imbalances that are discussed in *Path Notes* and *Shadow Strategies*.

The long-term goal is to learn to pray unceasingly and hopefully receive the gift of pure prayer and see the "uncreated light." It is an important distinction that the Christian who is saying this prayer is actually begging the "very Son of God, the Second Person of the Trinity, the Uncreated Word of God, Jesus Christ," for mercy. A fundamental distinction often lost between Christianity and Eastern religions is that Christians believe in a personal God, who became exclusively incarnate in Jesus, and the Eastern religions take the same position nondiscriminately. Mercy in this sense means considerably more than just the suspension of justice.

The physical techniques that are recorded, and there are advanced ones passed down from spiritual father to child, vary considerably. There are several positions used. We will just discuss the seated, for which a low stool is recommended. The back is straight and supple, the pelvis tilted lightly forward, while the neck is kept straight so the chin is tucked. In this position, the eyes should be focused on the heart. Not only do various writers warn about focusing on the belly or the lower centers, but they specify that the focus should be on the upper part of the physical heart, lest the focal point cause distraction, *prelest*, or illness. (In *chi kung* meditative arts the sitting stance and breath are the same, but with a visualization of a steaming kettle in the midriff. Focusing on the genitals, navel, or solar plexus has medical implications, but serious practitioners eventually focus attention on the upper chakra system or heart, throat, and head. Lower chakra for fighting, upper chakra for wisdom. The breathing techniques can influence the energy and hormonal balance of the practitioner.) The eyes are to remain closed and any form of visualization is actively avoided. (Martial visions are not to be ignored or avoided, but accepted.)

Orthodox theology strongly emphasizes the mystery of God, and attempting to visualize things leads quickly to *prelest*. *Prelest* is a Russian term that means delusion but implies much more. It suggests a falling away, a being lost, a deep confusion, as well as being deceived. Breathing varies, but the Orthodox are told to breathe not boldly but gently, and to not breathe at their ease. Some writers say the stomach is kept firm. The prayer is then said in various patterns with the breath. The most common practice is "Lord Jesus Christ,

Son of God" on the inhale with "have mercy on me, a sinner!" on the exhale. Sometimes the first part of this mantra is split into an inhalation and hold. The in/out pattern is also used while one is doing manual labor. Ideally one reaches the point where the prayer is unceasingly repeated in one's heart. One should note that "heart," like breath above, is a poor translation for a technical term in Greek and has metaphysical meanings as well as physical. Somewhat like the Japanese *shin*.

Somatrophic techniques are used that sound very similar to Taoist mediations. In the instructions to hesychasts, one finds: "As you breathe in, follow the breath with your mind until it reaches the heart. Let the mind remain there as you exhale." This is described as difficult and requiring much effort initially. The monastic life of the hesychast was difficult and violent to the ego. The scriptural passage "storming and taking hold with violence" is often used as a description of the monks' life, as is "working out salvation with fear and trembling."

Pure prayer and the vision of the "light of Tabor" are considered gifts and are not expected as a result of the physical technique. One writer claims that the physical techniques can ruin your lungs and make you insane if done without a teacher. The experience of a vision of the "uncreated light" only comes after purification, humility, repentance, and always as a free gift. Boredom is often the least of the problems of a monk. One should note that the breathing techniques used by the Orthodox monks were chosen to help one focus on the Prayer of the Heart. This not to say the Prayer of the Heart is not done by laymen; it was and still is. Hesychasm, however, implies a monastic life.

The breathing techniques of the martial arts were chosen to enhance ones' abilities by the strengthening of one's *chi*. Careful study of either system will find techniques rejected because they do not lead to the desired destination. Despite the differences between the hesychast and the internal martial artist's goals, surprisingly both find the same barrier to advancement. A monk is constantly warned against self-will and pride! A large chunk of the inability to benefit from or comprehend subtle energy is also related to pride. Study this well.

Sayings of Sentience
Arranged by Glenn Morris

"Do not consciously seek enlightenment,"
Muso Kokushi said.

"Meditate on knowing and not knowing,
Existing and not existing. Then leave both aside
So that you can be," Shiva said.

"Meditation is not the means to an end.
It is both the means and the end," J. Krishnamurti said.

"Don't read the scriptures. Practice meditation.
Don't take up the broom. Practice meditation.
Don't plant tea seeds. Practice meditation," Ikkyu said.

"At the point when sleep has not yet come
And wakefulness vanishes, being is revealed," Shiva said.

And you still aren't playing with this? Enough said.

Bibliography

Chapter One

H. R. Ellis Davidson, *The Sword in Anglo-Saxon England.* The Boydell Press, 1994. A history of technique, technology, and literature concerning the sword in the days of yore, before the Normans invaded and spoiled everything with their prissy ways.

Historic Reprints, at patri@dragonsys.com. A picture can be worth a thousand words.

J. Clements, *Renaissance Swordsmanship,* Paladin Press, 1997. Mr. Clements has rekindled interest in Western sword techniques and has developed a ferocious reputation in the Society for Creative Anachronism world as a duelist. I've crossed swords with some of his friends and it can be scary.

Hammervatz Forum, P.O. Box 13448, Baltimore, MD 21203. Has a fine magazine devoted to articles concerning Western swordsmanship.

George Silver, "Paradoxes of Defense" in *Three Elizabethan Fencing Manuals.* Scholar's Facsimiles and Reprints, 1972.

There is an old post Civil War collection of newspaper articles and writings titled *Sparks from the Campfire,* that preserved battle stories from both sides and will make one think. It may be out of print. I read a tattered, leather bound copy when I was a kid and was fascinated.

J. Gilbey, *Western Boxing and World Wrestling,* North Atlantic Books, 1986. Mr. Gilbey seldom fails to delight and amuse.

Paul. R. Buitron, *Encyclopedia of Savate Danse de Rue*, available through the author at Texas Association of Savate, 220 Hillside Rd. Laredo, Tx. 78041. (www.savatedansederue.com) This will probably be the preferred work on savate in English, and once it is translated into French it will continue to be outstanding. Many nasty things.

Michael Coe, et al., *Swords and Hilt Weapons*, Barnes and Noble, 1993. From the Stone Age to World War II we can see the development worldwide of pointy and edged tools to make people leak.

S. Matthew Galas, *Kindred Spirits: The Art of the Sword in Germany and Japan*. Journal of Asian Martial Arts. Volume 6, number 3, 1997. A very interesting article that clearly shows that great minds think alike, particularly when trying to kill each other. Pay close attention to where the feet are positioned in the old pictures.

Chapter Two

Jane Huang with Michael Wurmbrand, *The Primordial Breath (Vol. 1)*. Original Books. Seven treatises from the Taoist Canon, Tao Tsang translated to be tried out. Interesting interpretation of Lao Tzu as a guide to breath and meditation.

George A. Katchmer, *The Tao of Bioenergetics*. YMAA Publication Center. The best synthesis, paradigm-smashing, and shifting of scientific models East and West concerning energy work and hard science I've read. Freud, Reich, and Jung smacked into Lao Tzu, Confucius, and Mao with a bunch of philosophers and physicists to add leaven to a yeasty discussion. Fun to read if you are open-minded enough to handle it.

John White, ed, *Kundalini: Evolution and Enlightenment*. Paragon House. Kundalini research: first-hand accounts of arousal, commentary, and essays on this controversial subject. Western as well as Eastern perspectives.

Dr. Bonnie Greenwell, *Energies of Transformation: A Guide to the Kundalini Process*. Shakti River Press, 1990. 10311 DeAnza Blvd,

Cupertino, CA 95014. One of the best syntheses of Eastern and Western perspectives on kundalini phenomena. If you meditate, this book should be in your library as well as in your mind.

H. H. Wu, editor and Lheng Ping, translator, *Therapeutic Breath Exercises*. Hai Feng Publishing Company. Easy to learn self-training exercises for the chi kung enthusiast drawn from traditional Chinese medicine.

Robert W. Smith, "Breathing in Taiji and Other Martial Arts," *Journal of Asian Martial Arts*, Vol. 5. No. 4, 1996. Not one of Smith's better literary contributions to the art.

Tom Muncy, Rick Moneymaker, Rusy McMains, and Michael Davis, *Torite Jutsu Reference Manual*. Dragon Society International. Northshore Communications, 1997. www.dragonsociety.com or 1–888-torite-1. The martial artists' guide to pressure points, karate, TCM energy work, and other nasty things. Tell 'em Dr. Morris sent you to them.

James M. Robinson (General Editor), *The Nag Hammadi Library*. HarperCollins, Harper San Francisco. So you want to know about early Christianity? This is the most important translation of the Dead Sea Scrolls and the only complete one-volume version in English.

Chapter Three

Anthony Storr, *Feet of Clay: A Study of Gurus*. The Free Press 1230 Ave. of the Americas, New York, NY. 1996. (London, HarperCollins) Storr puts many in their psychiatric place. He misses a lot, as his hammer is heavy, but he drives some ferocious stakes into the heart of the vampires and knocks about some of those who are normally perceived as the good guys.

Yamamoto Tsunetomo, (translated. by William Scott Wilson), *Hagakure: The Book of the Samurai*. Avon/Discus. The story of one samurai told in his own words. Often quoted, seldom analyzed in depth. An interesting read that inspires many for reasons I find difficult to grasp.

John Douglas, *Journey into Darkness* and *Mindhunter.* Pocket Books. Mr. Douglas is a profiler of serial criminals for the FBI and can be very interesting and insightful in cataloguing how we can go wrong.

Kyriacos C. Markides, *Riding with the Lion.* Penguin/Arkana. In search of mystical Christianity, Markides finds some orthodox practices that will seem familiar to some readers and amazing to others.

Steven Pinker, Ph. D, *How the Mind Works.* Norton, New York/London, 1997. Witty and funny. Good read. A text that teaches you how to tune the most important engine in your life and why.

Chapter Four

Jeremy Hayward, *Sacred World: A Guide to Shambhala Warriorship in Daily Life.* Rider Books, London, 1975. Tibetan Buddhism for the twenty-first century. A good read full of technique and insight. His insights, explanations, and exercises are the best I have seen and that includes some Rinpoche writings. Were I you, I would study on this book particularly if you liked *Path Notes.*

Roy F. Baumeister, Ph.D, *Evil: Inside Human Violence and Cruelty.* W. H. Freeman & Company, 1997. A scary book: the basic premise is that ordinary people driven by circumstance will act in horrific ways. The majority of people who commit mass murders seem terribly conventional or normal.

Dr. John E. Upledger, *Your Inner Physician and You.* North Atlantic Books. 1991. Craniosacral Therapy is something you should try if you run into energy problems concerned with skull and spine.

Chapter Five

Thomas Cleary, *The Essential Tao: An Initiation into the Heart of Taoism Through the Authentic Tao Te Ching and the Inner Teachings of Chuang-tzu.* Castle Books, 1998. Cleary's bold translation opens the Chinese to the Western mind and provides some surprising twists to the familiar.

Dr. Masaaki Hatsumi, *Sanmyaku*. The bujinkan densho/newsletter can be had for $45.00 for six sporadic issues out of PO Box 30338, Stockton, CA 95213. Why not hear it from the horse's mouth? A newsletter chock full of tidbits of ninja lore. Back issues available.

Stephen Russell and Jurgen Kolb. *The Tao of Sexual Massage*. A Gaia Book. Fireside/Simon & Schuster, 1992. Next to the big red book, this should be by your bedside.

Chapter Six

Jane Huang with Michael Wurmbrand, *The Primordial Breath*. Original Books, Torrance, California. 1987. Ms. Huang translates seven treatises from the Taoist Canon (*Tao Tsang*) concerning prolonging life through breath control. The translation is quite good; her strength is understanding the medical applications. A literalist could easily be led astray by these wily words.

David R. Kinsley, *The Sword and the Flute*. University of California Press, Berkeley, 1975. Hindu mythology comes alive in the dark visions of the terrible and sublime Kali and Krisna.

Thomas Cleary, *The Inner Teachings of Taoism*. Shambhala, Boston & London, 1986. The major secrets of Taoist alchemy without the codes and cryptic images. This is a very valuable book if you are really going to follow your breath.

Chapter Seven

Dr. Yang, Jwing-Ming, *The Essence of Shaolin White Crane Martial Power and Qigong*. YMAA Publication Center, Jamaica Plain, MA. If you want to better understand how *chi kung* can benefit your practice of the martial arts as well as personal health, Dr. Yang provides an excellent cookbook. Interesting commentary on effects of *chi* development. A valuable book.

Dr. Thomas Cleary, *The Human Element*. Shambhala, Boston & London. A collection of wisdom and pithy sayings elucidating leadership principles.

Frederic & Maryann Brusatt, *Spiritual Literacy: Reading the Sacred in Everyday Life*. Scribner, New York. Enmeshed in the web of everyday life, this collection of readings is a layered learning experience for sensing wisdom.

Alice Feinstein and editors of Prevention Magazine, *Training the Body to Cure Itself: How to Use Exercise to Heal*. Rodale Press, 1992. Get serious. Why not get more benefit from your workout than washboard abs? We are all getting older. This book will help you hide it better. For those who think they know about exercise, I guarantee this book will widen your expertise.

Robert M. Giller, M.D. (& Kathy Matthews), *NATURAL Prescriptions*. Carol Southern Books, New York, 1994. So you don't trust TCM and want your medicine Western but not intrusive? Dr. Giller will walk you through the most common diseases that can be cured through food, vitamins, and supplements. To paraphrase Ben Franklin, a little prevention now can save you major problems later.

Maria Mercati, *The Handbook of Chinese Massage*. Healing Arts Press, Rochester, Vermont. The *chi* points, meridians, how and what is affected and why. A very useful book for the healer who needs good recipes and the poison hand practitioner who wants to know what he or she just ruined.

Chapter Eight

Ellen J. Langer, Ph.D, *The Power of Mindful Learning*. Addison Wesley, New York, 1997. So you want to learn to teach and write in a way that people will not only be helped but will remember what you said? Dr. Langer is an authority, both original and liberating. Put this one on your must-study list.

James Redfield, *The Celestine Vision*. Warner Books, New York, 1997. This is a better book than his earlier works. Through a merging of Eastern and Western methodologies and a concern for individual sychronicities, Mr. Redfield leads us optimistically to a spiritual convergence resulting in a better world.

Robert Ornstein, *The Right Mind: Making Sense of the Hemispheres.* Harcourt & Brace, New York, NY. Brain function and spirituality from a scientific perspective.

Peter Ralston, *The Art of Effortless Power: Cheng Hsin T'ui Shou.* North Atlantic Books, Berkeley, CA, 1991. Sifu/sensei Ralston has done a remarkable job of integrating some of the better physical techniques and philosophies of the martial arts.

Jay Gluck, *Zen Combat and The Secret Power Called Ki.* Personally Oriented Books, Ahiya, Japan, 1996. This is the revised edition of *Zen Combat* and the revision is well worth waiting for. Gluck-sensei has been a cartoonist and martial aficionado since the fifties; he brings rare insight to his discussion of personalities, events, and places. He knew many of the famous budoka of the past era and expresses his disappointment in some telling cases. Many of our heroes are better thought about from a distance.

The Warrior's Hand. Newsletter published by shinjinkan. $24.00 a year. One of the best martial arts newsletters around. Full of useful stuff instead of advertising. shinjink@maas.net or 318-491-9579. Published monthly.

Dr. Wayne W. Dyer, *Manifest Your Destiny.* Harper Collins, New York. The author of *Your Erroneous Zones.* Dumbed-down mysticism, but vocabulary and directions are useful.

Chapter Nine

Mihaly Csikszentmihalyi, *Flow: The Psychology of Optimal Experience.* New York: Harper and Row, 1990. Interviews of diverse populations of highly successful people who have had their moments of grace analyzed until the key elements of peak experience are scientized into a replicable process. Knowing this stuff can speed your process.

Tanmaya Honervogt,*The Power of Reiki.* Henry Holt, NY, 1998. A very useful book. Should be read by most of the reiki practitioners

I know. You will see and learn much from this book as it is well illustrated.

David Morehouse, *Psychic Warrior*. A young officer gets trained in out-of-body techniques and doesn't have a very good time.

Judith Orloff, MD, *Second Sight*. Warner Books, New York, NY, 1996. An interesting book. She tells her experience with a certain medical objectivity.

Daniel Reed, *The Tao of Health, Sex, and Longevity*. Simon and Schuster, 1995. If you are still struggling with Taoist concepts, this presentation is remarkably clear.

Daniel Reed,*Guarding the Three Treasures*. Simon and Shuster, 1993. Reed explains the basic *chi kung* techniques in clear lucid language. A book you will treasure.

Chapter Ten

A. T. Mann and Jane Lyle, *Sacred Sexuality*. Element Books, 1996. Beautiful graphics, prehistory to the present.

John Rowan, *The Horned God*. Routledge, London and New York, 1989. Feminism in perspective; nice discussion of androgyny from a Celtic perspective.

Bruce Bower, "Visions on the Rocks: Rock and cave art may offer insights into shamans' trance states and spiritual sightings." *Science News*, VOL. 150. October 5, 1996. Mr. Bower sums up the situation in a nice easy to read piece of journalism.

Ken Cohn, *The Way of Chi Kung*. Ballentine, 1997. A serious researcher. Easy to read, good science. There is a veritable encyclopedia of good stuff in this book.

Chapter Eleven

Phillip St. Romain, *Kundalini Energy and Christian Spirituality: A Pathway to Growth and Healing*. Crossroad Publishing, New York, 1994. Compelling testimony that even Roman Catholics can receive and achieve higher consciousness through prayer. The spontaneous awakening in a nice guy who wasn't doing *chi kung* or yoga and suddenly found himself to be an unexpected laboratory for the investigation of one of the most crucial questions that face modern Christians.

Richard Schulties and Robert Hofman, *Plants of the Gods: Their Sacred, Healing, and Hallucinogenic Powers.* Healing Arts Press, Rochester, Vermont, 1992. The title says it well. Has lots of pictures to help with identification. Some of the side effects may cramp your style.

Daniel P. Reid, *Chinese Herbal Medicine.* Shambhala, Boston, 1987. Tasty beneficial recipes in the back and a bunch of useful techniques in the front.

Any book about Hsing-I, Chinese Mind-Body Boxing , Chinese Internal Boxing, Pa Kua, or Chinese Boxing for Fitness and Self-defense. Jou Tsung Hwa in the *Tao of Tai-chi Chuan* talks about the mixing of the heaven and earth breath as well as cycles. Dr. Yang Jwing-Ming's books on the *Root of Chinese Chi-Kung* and *Muscle/Tendon Changing* contain detailed translations of the classics and use the same definition of "breath" as does J. Johnson's *The Master's Manual of Pa Kua.* Any description of circulating or moving the breath is biologically inaccurate as the lungs work like bellows. Most books on Shing Yi Chuan or Hsing I Chuan emphasis the physical and martial applications. A good one in English is *Xing Yi Quan Xue* by Sun Lu Tang or *Hsing I Chuan* by Liang Shou-Yu. No book exists yet on Gong style Shing Yi Chuan. Some exercises are similar to those described in M. Chia's *Iron Shirt Chi Kung.* For example, see Mantak Chia's *Awaken the Healing Tao, Fusion of the Five Elements,* and *Bone Marrow Nei Kung,* Li Ding's *Meridian Qigong,* Hua-Ching Ni's *Mastering Chi,* and Ken Cohen's extensive articles.

Concerning Orthodoxy, the *Philokalia* (Love of Beauty) has had the first four of its five volumes translated by Palmer, et al. and published in the last few years. In addition, several abstractions from it such as *Writings on Prayer from the Philokalia* and *Writings on The Prayer of the Heart,* have also been published. This collection of texts on prayer, meditation, and the life of the hesychast was developed over centuries to preserve the source materials used by the monks of Athos and other Orthodox centers. It contains texts dating back to the 4th century. John Climacus' *Ladder of Divine Ascent* is another core text. Recently other writers have discussed the same approach under the name of *The Prayer of the Heart.* Available in English are E. Behr-Sigel's *The Place of the Heart,* P. Velichkovsky's *The Scroll,* L. Gillet's *The Jesus Prayer,* and A. Goettmenn's *Prayer of Jesus* and *The Spiritual Wisdom and Practices of Early Christianity.* In addition, I. Brianchaninov's *On the Prayer of Jesus* has been retranslated. See both the writings of Theoplan the Recluse in *Writings on The Prayer of the Heart from the Philokalia* as well as Brianchaninov (cited above). See Brianchaninov's *The Arena* for a discussion of the monastic life.

About the Author

Glenn Morris is the author of *Path Notes of an American Ninja Master* and *Shadow Strategies of an American Ninja Master,* both published by North Atlantic Books. He earned a Ph.D. in Communication and Rhetoric from Wayne State University and has taught in many colleges and universities. For many years he has been a psychological consultant to industry, teaching and designing training programs in leadership development. He is an eighth-degree black belt in *togakure ryu ninpo taijutsu.* Vice president and owner of Pathobiotek Diagnostics, a publicly traded corporation, he lives in Houston, Texas.

Meditation Mastery, a series of eight audio tapes and manual, and *Advanced Hoshintao Chi Kung Meditations,* two audio tapes to enhance *chi kung* development, are available from the author at 713/939-1833, ext. 301.

For products and seminars by Glenn Morris: www.hoshin.com.